Dance in Scripture

art for faith's sake series

SERIES EDITORS:

Clayton J. Schmit
J. Frederick Davison

This series of publications is designed to promote the creation of resources for the church at worship. It promotes the creation of two types of material, what we are calling primary and secondary liturgical art.

Like primary liturgical theology, classically understood as the actual prayer and practice of people at worship, primary liturgical art is that which is produced to give voice to God's people in public prayer or private devotion and art that is created as the expression of prayerful people. Secondary art, like secondary theology, is written reflection on material that is created for the sake of the prayer, praise, and meditation of God's people.

The series presents both worship art and theological and pedagogical reflection on the arts of worship. The series title, *Art for Faith's Sake,*ⁱ indicates that, while some art may be created for its own sake, a higher purpose exists for arts that are created for use in prayer and praise.

* *Art for Faith's Sake* is a phrase coined by art collector and church musician, Jerry Evenrud, to whom we are indebted.

Dance in Scripture

*How Biblical Dancers Can
Revolutionize Worship Today*

Angela Yarber

CASCADE *Books* • Eugene, Oregon

DANCE IN SCRIPTURE
How Biblical Dancers Can Revolutionize Worship Today

Art for Faith's Sake 11

Cascade Books
An Imprint of Wipf and Stock Publishers
199 W. 8th Ave., Suite 3
Eugene, OR 97401

www.wipfandstock.com

ISBN 13: 978-1-62032-662-6

Cataloging-in-Publication data:

Angela Yarber.

Dance in scripture : how biblical dancers can revolutionize worship today / Angela Yarber.

Art for Faith's Sake 11

x + 116 p.; 23 cm—Includes bibliographical references and index.

ISBN 13: 978-1-62032-662-6

1. Religious dance. 2. Worship in the Bible. I. Title. II. Series.

GV1783.5 Y25 2012

Manufactured in the USA.

Dedicated to:
The memory of Walter Harrelson
It was an honor to call myself your pastor.

Table of Contents

Acknowledgments

While I may not have been aware of it at the time, the foundations of this book began to take shape in 2003. When I was an undergraduate writing my senior thesis about the role of dance in Christianity, my advisor, mentor, and dear friend Doug Weaver encouraged and supported me along the way. It is because of the guidance, love, and support of the entire Weaver family—Doug, Pat, Aaron, and Andrea—that I took the steps toward becoming a scholar in the first place. Portions of the chapters on Miriam and Jephthah's daughter also took shape some time ago. Namely, under the guidance of Nancy deClaissé-Walford, I wrote a master's thesis on the role of women in ancient Israelite dance. The way she emboldened me to write academically and to love the translation of Hebrew is a gift I will always savor. When I graduated seminary and headed west to pursue a PhD in Art and Religion, it was my beloved seminary professors who reminded me not to forsake my love of Scripture and to unabashedly research its connections with dance and the arts.

This book truly took shape upon teaching two courses about its contents, however. The first was a course about embodying the feminine divine where Andrea Bieler mentored me as I taught seminary students at the Pacific School of Religion. In the first half of this class, we explored all of the dancers in this book. Upon accepting the call to be Pastor for Preaching and Worship at Wake Forest Baptist Church, I taught another class, "Dance in Scripture," to congregants and community members who gathered once a week for a semester. Foremost among those gathered was Walter Harrelson. While he was one of the most well-respected scholars of the Hebrew Bible and likely already knew everything I could possibly teach in this class, he attended regularly and enthusiastically. Each week, he would take a seat on the front row and eagerly pipe, "What are we going to learn today, Professor?" I'll never forget the day when the class struggled with the "so what" question I always ask at the close of the session to prompt us all to consider how what we have learned may impact our daily lives and faith. Walter responded, "Dance is what makes the Torah more bearable." So it is.

When the class concluded, Walter invited me to join him for lunch and strongly encouraged me to seek publication for the material I covered in class. In fact, he offered to write the foreward for the book because he believed in the importance of the project. I was honored, excited, and humbled. When the wonderful people at Cascade Books offered me a contract to publish this book, Walter became more and more ill. The same week they sent me a contract for Walter to sign for his foreward, he passed away peacefully at a hospice. So, this book is dedicated to his memory and the way he taught so many to love the translation of Scripture with grace, enthusiasm, and humility. The fact that such a brilliant mind had such a gracious heart never ceases to amaze me. He never spoke with the arrogance or elitism the academy often offers, but instead with kindness, humor, and compassion. I was truly honored to call myself his pastor during our time together at Wake Forest Baptist Church. Readers will notice the epigraph in Chapter 1 is Walter's phrase. It seemed appropriate to let him have the first words. Annotations are provided for subsequent epigraphs except for Chapters 4 and 6, which are my own words.

There are still others in need of acknowledgment. For Diane Farley and Christian Amondson and their work at Cascade Books, I am grateful. For the scholarship of Phyllis Trible, Toni Craven, and Athalya Brenner, whose feminist exegesis paved the way for books like this, I am grateful. For Diane Apostolos-Cappadona, who continues to be a forerunner in the field, a friend, and mentor, I am grateful. For a family who supports my wacky writing schedules, I am grateful. And for a brilliant, beautiful, gentle, compassionate, peacemaking partner, Elizabeth, who proofreads, listens to me process, and makes me laugh every day, I am profoundly grateful. It is because of all of you that this book became a reality. Thank you.

CHAPTER 1

Introductions

Dance is what makes the Torah more bearable.

—WALTER HARRELSON

Emma Goldman is famously remembered for saying, "If I can't dance, I don't want to be a part of your revolution." Like the myriad revolutionaries who danced before her, Goldman's pithy statement epitomizes the agency of the dancing body in bringing about social change, standing for justice, and revolutionizing worship today. Like Goldman, I find that dance and revolution are inextricably linked. Accordingly, in this book I seek to tell the stories of the Bible's dancing characters and how their dances have the power to revolutionize worship today.

Many of their stories lurk in the neglected crevices of the canon, rarely appearing in the lectionary and even less frequently read aloud or preached in worship. In the same way that the body, and specifically the dancing body, is often neglected or ignored in Christian worship, so too are the biblical texts that describe the importance of the body in worship. Such is the case with Jephthah's dancing daughter, the Shulamite, Judith, or Jesus' dance. Others are known but frequently misunderstood. In the same way that the body, and specifically the dancing body, is often misunderstood in Christian worship, so too are the biblical texts that are habitually poorly interpreted and exegeted through the lens of an anti-body bias. Such is the case with David or Salome. What might happen to our worship today if we celebrated and embodied these stories of biblical dancers rather than negating or ignoring them? How might our worship change for the better if we allowed our bodies to join our hearts, minds, and voices in the same way that these biblical dancers did? Who are the biblical dancers that have the power to revolutionize worship today?

Dance in Scripture: How Biblical Dancers Can Revolutionize Worship Today proposes that understanding the virtues embodied by the dances of seven biblical figures can revolutionize worship and ritual in today. This book details the role of dance in the bible by seven dancing figures: Miriam, Jephthah's daughter, David, the Shulamite, Judith, Salome, and Jesus. Combined with a thorough exegesis of the texts, each figure teaches contemporary readers about the primacy of embodiment and dance in worship and ritual. Further, every unique figure highlights the way that dance can be used to express particular virtues. Miriam's dance embodies the virtue of liberation; Jephthah's daughter's dance embodies the virtue of lamentation; David's dance embodies the virtue of abandon; the Shulamite's dance embodies the virtue of passion; Judith's dance embodies the virtue of subversion; Salome's dance embodies the virtue of innocence; and Jesus' dance embodies the virtue of community. The exegetical understanding of each dancing text combines with the virtues they embody to produce models for contemporary readers to address these virtues within the context of worship today. These ancient dancers have the potential of teaching contemporary readers how to use dance to embody virtues that will revolutionize worship and ritual.

Biblical Words for Worship, Praise, and Dance

Before digging deeper into the stories of these ancient dancers, it is important first to review briefly the Hebrew and Greek words for worship, praise, and dance. Mayer Gruber contends that "the high level of interest and development in choreography can be noted by the fact that the Bible has eleven verb forms to describe dancing."[1] It also worth noting that the words traditionally translated as "worship" or "praise" literally have kinesthetic meanings, thus indicating the ingrained importance of movement and embodiment in Israelite worship. Primary to the understanding of the embodied nature of many Hebrew words is the work of Mayer Gruber and Julian Morganstern. Their works regarding words for dance in the Hebrew Bible are unprecedented.

The Hebrew Bible describes worship in physical terms. Throughout Scripture one finds a variety of physical postures associated with worship:

---

1. Gruber, "Ten Dance-Derived Expressions," 48.

lying prostrate, lifting hands, standing, kneeling, clapping, lifting or bowing the head, and dancing. Worship, for the ancient Hebrews, is appropriately physical. *Yadah* is translated as "praise," such as in Psalm 134:2, "praise God in the sanctuary and bless the Lord." However, *yadah* literally means "to confess with outstretched hands."[2] *Yadah* incorporates the Hebrew word for hand (*yod*), implying the "stretching out or holding out of the hands, and possibly the pointing, throwing, casting, extending or shooting out of the hands."[3] In a similar vein is another Hebrew word for praise, *barak*. *Barak* is translated as "praise" over seventy times in the Hebrew Bible. Yet *barak* literally indicates kneeling, blessing, praising, or saluting.[4] Thus, the words that are translated as praise actually have embodied connotations.

Another important word in the discussion of the embodiment of worship is the word *shachah*. One finds the word worship translated over 170 times in the Hebrew Bible. Yet worship for the ancient Israelites did not occur in their hearts and minds alone but manifested itself in the entire body. Thus, *shachah* can be translated literally as "to bow, sink down, to depress, to bow down, to prostrate oneself, to worship, to adore."[5] The verb occurs in the Hithpael, the reflexive stem, which indicates that the action performed is reciprocated; as one bows down to God, God bows down in return. Just as praise indicates a bodily response, so too does the notion of worship. This idea is a key concept in ancient Israelite worship. For the ancient Israelites, the body and soul were not mutually exclusive. Rather, worship and praise were embodied in prayer, motion, gestures, dance, and music.

What is more, the concept of dance was ingrained in Israelite worship. "Dance lives at the heart of the Hebrew Scriptures; there is scarcely a chapter that does not have at least an indirect relationship to dance."[6] The prominence of dance is noted primarily in the fact that there are so many different Hebrew verbs to describe dancing. The survey of nine of these verbs relies upon the work of Mayer Gruber's "Ten Dance-Derived Expressions in the Hebrew Bible,"[7] which utilizes the following criteria to determine translation: (a) when a particular verb is employed literally or juxtaposed with

---

2. Hibbert, *Prophetic Worship*, 67.

3. Ibid.

4. Ibid., 66.

5. Feyerabend, *Hebrew Dictionary*, 345–46.

6. DeSola, *The Spirit Moves*, 95.

7. The next nine words discussed in this study all come from Gruber, "Ten Dance-Derived Expressions," 48–66.

other expressions denoting physical acts; (b) the determination of semantic equivalents in biblical Hebrew and cognate languages; (c) traditions preserved in talmudic literature; and (d) comparisons with terminology employed in other cultures whose dance has been systematically investigated.

The first word for dance is *hagag*, which can be translated as "dance in a circle." Thirteen of the sixteen occurrences of this verb in the Hebrew bible mean simply "celebrate." The most plausible explanation as to how a single verb can mean "dance in circles (as though one was drunk)" and "celebrate" is that the verb *hagag*—whose basic meaning is "move about in a circle"—was used to refer to dancing in a circle in celebration of victory as perhaps in 1 Samuel 30:1 or Psalm 42:5.

The next verb worth considering is *sabab*, which can be translated as "encircle, turn about." Three attestations of *sabab* are Jeremiah 31:22; Psalm 114:3–5; and Ecclesiastes 12:5. The most obvious instance of *sabab* "encircle" that refers to dance is Psalm 26:6 where the psalmist says, "I shall wash my palms with innocence so that I may walk in the procession (*sabab*) around your altar, O Lord." Here *sabab* refers to the same rite of worship as described in 1 Samuel 30:16 by the verb *hagag*. In Psalm 114:3–4 are more usages of *sabab* referring to a dance performed as an act of divine worship. Jeremiah 31:22 *sabab* refers to the universal phenomenon of circumambulation of the bridegroom, bride, or bridal couple.

Raqad is the third verb that indicates a type of dance. It is typically translated as "skip." In the Jerusalem Talmud, Beza 5:1 *qippus* denotes removing both feet from the ground simultaneously, while *raqad* denotes removing one foot from the ground while placing the other foot upon the ground, conveying an idea of "skipping." It could be concluded, then, that David's dance before the ark in 1 Chronicles 15:29 was a skip dance. Scripture seems to characterize *raqad* as the activity of rams, calves, and goats. The similes "dance like a calf" in Psalm 29:6, "dance like rams" and "dance like young sheep" in Psalm 114:4–6 suggest that in ancient Israel *raqad* was regarded as an imitation of the skipping cattle. Because the dance is frequently a feature of mourning rites, it should not be surprising that in Syriac the root r-q-d came to have the two meanings "dance" and "mourn." In the Hebrew Bible, though, *raqad* is understood to be a dance of joy.

The fourth verb for dance is *qippus*, which is translated as "jump." As indicated above, both *raqad* and *qippus* were attested as terms designating specific and distinct dance forms during the Amoraic period. The Jerusalem Talmud sheds light on these dance forms; the one instance of *qippus*, however, in the Hebrew Bible, Song of Songs 2:8, does not refer to dance. Song of Songs 2:8 also indicates the role of a fifth verb, *dillug*, as a type of jumping dance, for it is employed as a synonym for *qippus* in Song of Songs 2:8. This reference helps us to appreciate the one reference to a jumping dance in the Hebrew Bible found in Isaiah 35:6, "then the lame will dance (*dillug*) like a hart, and the tongue of the dumb shall sing a joyous song." Here the parallelism "dance like a hart"/ "sing a joyous song" reflects the universal association of song and dance.

Kirker is yet another Hebrew word for dance that can be translated as "whirl, pirouette." The verb *kirker* is twice attested in the account of King David's dancing in the procession that brought the ark to Jerusalem in 2 Samuel 6:14, 16. The interpretation of *kirker* as a whirling dance is based primarily on the view that the form of *kirker* found in 2 Samuel 6 is an intensive of the verb for "rotate." *Kirker* is most likely the turning round and round upon the heels in one spot, as practiced by the dervishes. Equally plausible from an etymological point of view, and preferred by reasons of its antiquity, is the suggestion presented anonymously in Numbers Rabbah 4:20 that *kirker* designates "pirouette." The interpretation of *kirker* as "pirouette" is supported by numerous uses of the verb and derived nouns in Rabbinic Hebrew and in Ugaritic literature for denoting a gesture of the hand rather than a movement upon the heel or toe. If *kirker* may denote both dancing and a gesture of the hand, it could be plausible based on Sachs's delineation of sitting dances in which significant movements take place from the waist up and the hasta "single hand gesture" and the samyuta hasta "double hand gesture," which have now become the hallmark of Indian classical dance. One of the two biblical references to *kirker* as "whirling, pirouette" is 2 Samuel 6:14a, "David was whirling with all might before the Lord." The adverbial phrase "before the Lord" indicates that the dance was performed as an act of worship. *Kirker* is used again in 2 Sameul 6:16.

Yet another word of importance is *pizzez* which is translated as "skip." The verb *pizzez* is attested with reference to a dance step only in 2 Samuel 6:16. It is interpreted as such based on 1 Chronicles 15:29, which seems to equate the common *raqad* with the rare verb *pizzez* by substituting the former for the latter.

The eighth word for dance is *pasah*. *Pasah* is associated with a "limp dance." Some scholars suggest that the festival of Pesach derives its name from a limping dance performed during festival days in antiquity; they presume the noun is a derivation of the verb. In 1 Kings 18:26 the behavior of the priests of Baal is described as, "they performed a limping dance around the altar Elijah had made." Scholars contest that Elijah refers to a limping dance also in 1 Kings 18:21, "it is long enough that you are limping between two opinions." In this case the prophet is asking the people to perform a limping dance for the one deity or for the other, but not for both. These same scholars sometimes suggest that this type of dance is peculiar to the worship of Baal and foreign to the worship of Yahweh.

A final verb worthy of note prior to addressing an in-depth study of *mahol* is the Hebrew word *siheq*. *Siheq* can be translated as "dance, play." The piel form of *siheq* is most interesting to this study. In 2 Samuel 6:21 King David tells Michal that he intends to do more of that which he is described as having done in 2 Samuel 6:14. He says "I shall dance (*siheq*)," while in 6:14 he is described as doing a whirling dance (*kirker*). In most other cases, however, the piel form of *siheq* simply means play.

The origin of *mahol* is obscure, according to Podechard.[8] According to Julian Morgenstern, though, the "fundamental meaning of the stem *hol* is 'to revolve in a circle,' 'to turn,' while in Hebrew 'to dance' is the simplest meaning of the word."[9] He believes that the likelihood of the original meaning of this stem was "to be round," and from this the secondary meaning, "to revolve in a circle," "to turn" and "to dance," evolved.[10] It is striking that various words in Hebrew and other Semitic languages for "to be round" are similar to the words for "to dance." In this vein it is interesting to note that *hll*, "to pierce," 'to wound,' in other words 'to make a round hole,' which all modern lexicographers distinguish most carefully from *hll* 'to profane,' is a secondary formation from *hol* 'to be round.' This would account for the following derivatives: *mahol* a flute, i.e., an instrument through which a round hole (or holes) has (have) been pierced."[11]

Furthermore, "as a rule every vineyard in ancient Israel had a *mahol*, etymologically a 'dancing-place,' an open space from twelve to sixteen cubits in width, surrounding the entire vineyard between fence and vines."[12] Bertinoro notes that in this *mahol* the maidens of Israel used to celebrate their vineyard dances, implying the regular celebration of the annual

---

8. Gruber, "Ten Dance-Derived Expressions," 411.

9. Morgenstern, "The Etymological History," 321.

10. Ibid., 321.

11. Ibid., 322.

12. Ibid., 324.

festival when the women of Shiloh came forth to dance in the vineyards (Judg 20–21; 1 Kgs 19:16). The Mishna provides more detailed information:

> The maidens of Jerusalem used to go out, clad in white garments, that had been borrowed, in order not to put to shame those who had none. All these garments had to be previously dipped in water. And the maidens of Jerusalem would go out and dance in the vineyards. And what would they say? "Young man, lift thine eyes and see whom thou wilt choose. Set not thine eyes upon beauty, but upon the family" . . . The Mishna states very closely that these dances were celebrated twice each year . . . [This] indicates that in the ancient Israelite and pre-Israelite form of the ceremony the young men regularly stood by, openly or concealed in the vineyards, as were the Benjaminites, and at the proper moment stepped forth and seized, each the maiden of his choice, to become his partner in sacred sexual intercourse for the night, and his wife and the mother of his children for the future.[13]

From a feminist perspective this word usage could make some uncomfortable. There is, however, also goddess worship associated with these dances. Together with sacred sexual intercourse, these *mahol* dances, were "in origin undoubtedly homeopathic magical rites, celebrated in the worship of the ancient Semitic mother-goddess, and were designed to promote the fertility of vineyards and fields."[14] Thus, the term *mahol* is not so much related to "a woman who has been profaned" in a moral sense, as one who has participated in the sacred sexual intercourse attendant originally upon the dances.[15]

For these reasons it is apparent why Mayer Gruber states, "the most frequently attested and therefore most frequently discussed term for 'dance' in the Hebrew Bible is *mahol*."[16] *Mahol* was originally associated with dance on a joyous occasion and by extension also came to connote "joy." "It should not be surprising that of all the terms for 'dance' in biblical Hebrew the one that develops the nuance 'joy' is *mahol*, seeing that this is the type of dance which is danced as an expression of joy upon the safe return from battle of the armies of Israel . . . It is the association of *mahol* with military victory demonstrated in Judges 11:34; 1 Samuel 18:6–7, 21:12b and 29:5, as well

13. Quoted in ibid., 324–25.
14. Ibid., 327.
15. Ibid., 329.
16. Gruber, "Ten Dance-Derived Expressions," 56.

as Exodus 15:20."[17] The association of chanting (1 Sam 18:6) and *mahol* lends support to the theory developed by Jack Sasson that *mahol* is "both etymologically related to and a semantic equivalent of Akkadian *melultu*, which, in turn, corresponds to the Greek *hyporchema*, a multimedia performance including instrumental music, dance, choral singing, and mime."[18] Just as by synecdoche *mahol* came to be employed to designate "joy," the same term came to designate a musical instrument. The interpretation of the term *mahol* as the name of an instrument was advocated by the medieval philologists Ibn Janah, Abraham Ibn Ezra, and David Kimhi and in modern times by N. H. tur-Sinai.[19] J. S. Licht argues that *mahol* has two meanings. He holds that "dance" is appropriate in Judges and Exodus but "flute" is fitting in Psalm 149:3 and 150:4. "Perhaps, however, the noun *mahol*, which originally meant 'dance,' came to mean 'flute' or 'drum,' because it was used to provide music or rhythm for the dancing of dance called *mahol*."[20] Finally, *mahol* is also interpreted as a whirl dance in which the dancer rotates and "thereby exhibits her beauty" to prospective marriage partners.[21]

It is clearly evident that the ancient Hebrews were a kinesthetic people. Their words for worship and praise indicate a bodily response to God. In addition, the mass variety of words for dance indicates that they embodied their worship; dance was ingrained in the culture.

While not quite as prominent as in the Hebrew Bible, the Greek New Testament also offers a variety of terms that indicate the primacy of the body in worship. For example, one frequently translated as "worship" is *proskuneo*, which literally means "to bow down, bow low, do reverence to, worship." In the same way that *shachah* offers the embodied connotation of bowing in the Hebrew Bible, so too does *proskuneo* in the New Testament. Another fascinating term is *agallio*. *Agallio* is most often translated as "exceedingly glad," but literally has the connotation of "very much leaping." Its associations are similar to the concept of jumping for joy. When one is so overcome with joy, one's body often responds.

While these Hebrew and Greek word studies may seem exhausting on the surface, it is important to note what is often lost in translation. The

---

17. Ibid., 57.

18. Sasson, "The Worship of the Golden Calf," 157–59.

19. Gruber, "Ten Dance-Derived Expressions," 57.

20. Ibid., 58.

21. Ibid.

embodied connotations associated with the words for worship and praise are lost when translated into English. When a reader proclaims these words in worship today, rarely do congregants know that "Praise the Lord" could literally mean "confess with outstretched hands to the Lord" or "kneel before the Lord." Similarly, when we speak of worship from the pulpit by reading biblical texts, rarely does one respond with the literal embodied meaning of the word by prostrating or bowing. More often, we reserve worship and praise for the head, the heart, and the voice. By neglecting the body, however, worshipers are neglecting and forsaking our embodied worshiping history. If we claim that our worship is biblical, our bodies simply must move. Whether it is hands outstretched in praise, knees bowed in worship, or bodies dancing like Miriam, Jephthah's daughter, David, the Shulamite, Judith, Salome, or Jesus, it is our responsibility as worshipers to unite our body with our head and heart. This union of body, mind, and heart has the potential to revolutionize worship today.

In the pages that follow we will step inside the stories of these biblical dancers. Their stories are not only about incorporating dance and the body into worship. They also involve liberation, celebration, lamentation, grief, injustice, abandon, misunderstanding, love, passion, sensuality, subversion, innocence, sexism, vulnerability, and community. In other words, the stories of these biblical dancers are a lot like the stories of individuals and communities at worship. The stories are complicated, nuanced, and sometimes difficult to understand. The stories sometimes bring healing and sometimes bring pain. In each of these situations in life, there is dance. So, too, should there be in worship today. In fact, I would propose that dancing in the face of liberation, lamentation, abandon, passion, subversion, innocence, and community just might revolutionize worship today. And if I can't dance, I don't want to be a part of your revolution.

CHAPTER 2

Miriam's Dance: Liberation

Exodus 15:20

We are your subtlest instruments:
no music branches to your breast
that does not sound in us,
no music dies away from you,
that in us lives not,
and even in your absence
your cadence journeys . . .

—ALLEN MANDELBAUM, *CHELMAXIOMS*[1]

Often relegated to the submissive role of sister, the character of Miriam is typically overshadowed by the triumphs of her younger brother. Like many of her canonical contemporaries, Miriam receives little attention in Scripture. Her name is only mentioned twice and the story of her song is left unsung by the writers of Exodus. In order to understand how Miriam's dance of liberation can revolutionize worship today, it is vital to examine Miriam as a prophetess and dancer, place her dance in context, and recognize her contribution to Israelite dance.

Understanding the depth of Miriam's character is problematic since her story is given minimal attention in the Hebrew Bible. According to modern midrashic reading, the character development of most female characters is often quite truncated because both biblical writers and rabbinic traditions were shaped by patriarchy. We are left, then, with only pieces of

---

1. Cited in Hammer, *Sisters at Sinai*, 127.

information. According to Norman Cohen, if we believe "that the principle of egalitarianism is crucial, then it is incumbent upon us to attempt to piece together the isolated notes 'sung' by the women in the Bible, thereby recreating their lost songs."[2] Rather than understanding the character of Miriam as a supporting role in the Exodus drama, it is critical to recognize that Miriam was actually a starring player. Phyllis Trible suggests a careful reading of the Exodus event reveals Miriam as a mediator, a prophet, a dancer, and a leader of her people who "for a time probably shared power equally with her two brothers, Moses and Aaron."[3]

While her name is not mentioned when reading the story of the Egyptian women's discovery of Moses in Exodus 1, many scholars assume that the sister present is, indeed, Miriam. The tale of Moses' birth involves scandal, danger, and the faith of a frightened mother and daughter. Miriam's birth, however, involves no such story. She enters Scripture indirectly. "No lineage, birth announcement or naming-ritual proclaims her advent. Only silence gives her birth."[4] While she is given no naming-ritual, Miriam's name holds great meaning. Her name may be understood as an amalgam of two Hebrew words: *mar*, meaning "bitter," and *yam*, meaning "sea." These bitter waters usher forth the essence of Miriam's name: Rebellious Waters. Throughout her life, the flowing waters—much like a flowing dance—epitomize her relationship with the people of Israel. She is there delivering at the waters of Moses' birth. She is there dancing at the waters of the Reed Sea. And she is there serving at the waters of the well that bears her name. She represents the waters: life-giving, life-supporting, nourishing, and sustaining. Yet, according to Marsha Mirkin, "she is far from a passive nurturer. Miriam is a rebel, willing to confront injustice, willing to find the joy that is not-so-hidden in adversity."[5]

At the same time, her name, like Miriam, arose out of Egypt. For the name *Miriam* may also be derived from the Egyptian word *mer*, meaning "beloved."[6] Indeed, the people loved her, especially on account of the miraculous well which sustained them during their forty years in the wilderness.

> Since Miriam's whole life was associated with water, her very presence amongst the people was analogized to the existence of a well

2. Cohen, "Miriam's Song," 179.
3. Trible, "Bringing Miriam Out of the Shadows," 16.
4. Ibid., 18.
5. Mirkin, *The Women Who Danced*, 113–14.
6. Frankel, *The Five Books of Miriam*, 113.

which sustained Israel for forty years. The Rabbis saw her as the major redemptive vehicle for the people and symbolized her role by speaking of a miraculous well which provided water during the arduous journey from slavery to freedom. It was called "Miriam's well," and the water which flowed from it was said to have the taste of milk, wine and honey.[7]

Although Miriam's birth is given no great celebration, her life serves as a paradigm for the leading roles of women, of dancers, in a community whose true stories are often squelched by patriarchal writers. In fact, Miriam's only relation to men is that of sister. Unlike most women in Scripture, Miriam is never called a wife or mother. These attributes do not define her because she has neither husband nor children. It seems that androcentric tradition cannot tolerate her single status. In fact, the Jewish historian Josephus deems Hur the husband of Miriam.[8] Some midrashic material illustrates a degree of discomfort with Miriam's single status, as well. Rather than ascribing to her a husband, however, they relate her to the midwives, Shiphrah and Puah, noting that she waited patiently on the shores of the Nile in order to protect baby Moses. These early midrashic Rabbis equate Miriam with the midwives mentioned in the previous chapter of Exodus.[9]

Despite the neglect her story has suffered, the legacy of Miriam's dance continues because of the purity of her character. In the face of adversity and oppression, one can discover the liberation that Miriam's dance delivers. In the face of a Mosaic bias embedded in the text, Miriam's dance endures.[10] As we seek to discover the depth of Miriam's dance, we can hear her cry out:

> I am the Singer, the Dancer, the Drummer of Israel. I celebrate the myriad contributions of Jewish women through the ages. I champion their dreams, nurture their desires, encourage them in their spirits flag [sic]. When I was but a child of five, I chastised my father and all the Hebrew men for abandoning their marriage beds; when I was leader of our free people, I upbraided my brother Moses for abandoning his marriage bed. Mine is the voice of joy, of victory, of power. I prophesy the redemption of our people! My vision is clear and limitless. I see to the last generation![11]

7. Cohen, "Miriam's Song," 186.

8. Trible, "Miriam 1," 128.

9. Cohen, "Miriam's Song," 181.

10. Trible, "Bringing Miriam Out of the Shadows," 20.

11. Frankel, *The Five Books of Miriam*, xxii.

As the examination of Miriam's journey continues—her dance, her prophecy, her story, her contribution to Israel—may her character guide this investigation. May she always be remembered as a dancing "rebel in the footsteps of God, fearlessly promoting life."[12]

Miriam the Prophetess

Miriam is a prophetess; she is a sister; she is a dancer. The Torah defines her as nothing else.[13] While Miriam's role as a prophetess is not as important as her role as a dancer to the current study, it is still worthy of consideration, particularly because of its linkage to liberation. In Exodus 15:20, Miriam is named in the text for the first time. In this initial naming, she is also given a title: prophet. Accordingly, she is the first woman in all of Israel to bear this title, and she acquires it *before* her brother Moses.[14] Though the meaning of her title is indeterminate, Miriam is still the first woman to ever bear it. Just as Moses becomes the archetype of the male prophetic tradition, Miriam becomes the female archetype.[15] One might even argue that Miriam is the ultimate archetype of the entire prophetic tradition because she is given a title before Moses. Could it be that a dancing woman personifies what it means to be a prophet?

According to William Propp, the role of a prophet or prophetess is one that "transmits divine messages to humans."[16] Only four other women are described as prophets in the Hebrew Bible: Deborah (Judg 4:4), Huldah (2 Kgs 22:14), Nodadia (Nah 6:14), and Isaiah's anonymous wife (Isa 8:3). Perhaps Miriam's prophetic office is directly related to her musical performance; some scholars argue that all praise singers are prophets.[17] Might we argue that all dancers are prophets, as well?

While many scholars view Miriam's title as wholly valid, others highlight the association tied to the label. Rather than calling Miriam a prophetess, the writer deems it necessary to associate the woman's title to a man, namely her brother Aaron. At the same time, it is worth noting that it is not Moses' name that is attached to the title of prophetess. At the precise

---

12. Mirkin, *The Women Who Danced*, 115.

13. Ibid., 121.

14. Trible, "Bringing Miriam Out of the Shadows," 18.

15. Trible, "Miriam 1," 127.

16. Propp, *Exodus 1–18*, 546–47.

17 Ibid., 547.

moment when Moses performs his most-remembered miracle—parting the sea—Miriam is not associated with him but rather with his brother. It is Miriam, sister of Aaron, who dances on the shores of liberation and freedom.

Both Miriam's name and title appear for the first time during a pivotal moment in Miriam's life: her dance of liberation. Miriam is singled out from other women in the Hebraic tradition because she both dances and prophesies.[18] There are other dancers. There are other prophets. But she is the only biblical woman to do both. One may even propose that Miriam's title as prophetess and her role as a dancer are inextricably linked.

Miriam the Dancer

The only record of Miriam's dance is found in Exodus 15:20: "And Miriam, the prophetess, the sister of Aaron, went forth with a hand-drum in her hand, and all of the women went out after her with hand-drums and with dance."[19] Miriam may not proclaim prophetic words or issue prophetic warnings to the people of Israel, but Miriam's dance is her prophecy: "A prophet in the Jewish tradition is a messenger who brings God's will to the people. Miriam's message was coded in her timbrel. 'Dance, sing!' The music cries out, 'Do what finds favor in God's eyes. When there is a choice of life and death, choose life. At awe-inspiring moments, celebrate the moment, be grateful for it, find the blessing in it and recognize God in our celebration!'"[20]

At a moment when Miriam witnessed both freedom and oppression, liberation and bondage, joy and sorrow, death and life, she chose to dance. She chose to pause and create a ritual. The moment her feet hit dry land, Miriam opted to worship with dance. Her dance was accompanied by a song. In the paradoxical grip of God's freedom and fear, Miriam lifted her voice and moved her feet, proving that God's joy cannot be contained. Many scholars attribute her song in Exodus 15 to Moses; others contribute the melody to Miriam. According to Walter Brueggemann, "as the great rhetorical climax to this long tale of inversion, we are given a brief poem, commonly called 'The Song of Miriam.' This poem is regarded by scholars as being very old, perhaps the oldest Israelite poem we have and perhaps

18. Apostolos-Cappodona, "Scriptural Women Who Danced," 97.

19. Translation mine.

20. Mirkin, *The Women Who Danced*, 118.

composed very close to the time of these remembered events."[21] While Brueggemann and others subscribe the entirety of the song to Miriam, others believe that pieces belong to Miriam and pieces belong to Moses. Mirkin notes:

> After Miriam picks up her timbrel, she sings a short piece of a song that mimics the beginning of Moses' long song. *"Sing to YHVH, for He has triumphed gloriously; the horse and his rider has He thrown into the sea."* Some biblical scholars maintain that Miriam's longer, richer song is lost to us and this short piece is the only part that is saved. I envision Miriam differently. The Miriam whom I imagine is interested in bringing people to the point of dancing and creating their own songs. She reminds us with her words that it is our responsibility to honor God, to create songs and dances so that we can rejoice in the moment.[22]

It is difficult to decipher whether the entire song or only pieces should be attributed to Miriam. In light of these difficulties, it is apparent, however, that Miriam danced and sang. As she danced, the women followed her courageous lead and joined her song and dance. Songs of liberation and victory were typically limited to women in a manner similar to the way women exited their homes to greet men upon the return from battle. However, there was no need for Miriam to greet the male victors with dance because she, too, was a tremendous victor. As Cohen imagines: "One can almost picture that, as the people hurriedly gathered their possessions and fled Egypt in the middle of the night, Miriam called back to the other women, saying . . . 'don't forget the drums . . . we'll need them to celebrate our freedom.' As a matter of fact, the Midrash, in interpreting this passage, emphasizes that the righteous are always prepared for the moment of redemption."[23] In addition, some scholars feel that Miriam not only led the women in song and dance, but functioned as a leader of worship for all of the Israelites. The text says that Miriam sang responsively to "them." Yet, the Hebrew pronoun "them" is masculine, not feminine.[24] One may deduce, then, that Miriam led both men and women in a song and dance of liberation and freedom.

21. Brueggemann, "Exodus," 802.

22. Mirkin, *The Women Who Danced*, 118.

23. Cohen, "Miriam's Song," 182–83.

24. Trible, "Bringing Miriam out of the Shadows," 19.

While archeology and the biblical material are inextricably clear that women are associated with timbrels or hand-drums,[25] it is difficult to imagine Miriam and the women celebrating victory and excitement with dancing and song while the men stood idly by, watching their own liberation expressed on the heels and lips of women. Instead, one may assess that men probably could not help but join in the excitement as *all* the Israelites celebrated their newfound freedom. Breuggemann articulates beautifully Miriam's role as a dancer and leader of the people. While his thoughts are lengthy, they communicate perfectly the spirit of Miriam's dance and are worth noting as he states:

> The poem (song) is placed on the lips and in the dancing feet of Miriam and the Israelite women. We know elsewhere that there were women especially skilled in the singing required by the community for grief and death (Jeremiah 9:17; 2 Chronicles 35:25). In the same way, no doubt there were women, perhaps the same ones, skilled in singing and dancing with joy and exultation for liberation, victory, and well-being. The OT lets us see a community that is easily and readily evoked into the "surplus" activity of liturgy for the emotional, political extremities of joy and grief, well-being and loss. It may be that at the exodus itself there was such singing and dancing, such glad release of stifled yearning, such freedom for which bodies in Israel had long ached . . . There is no doubt that as the exodus liberation became a stylized liturgical event, this song and its unfettered dancing must have become standard practice. It is the liturgical remembering and hoping of every community of the oppressed that catches a glimpse of freedom and authorizes liturgical exaggeration to say, "Free at last!" . . . Now the story of Miriam and the women is placed as the ultimate verdict of Israel's faith.[26]

In these ways it is Miriam, the dancing prophetess, who inaugurates a custom, who codifies ritual, who embodies her worshiping tradition in her dance. With a song of gratitude on her lips, she begins to dance on the shores of freedom. The others cannot help but join her, their bodies whirling in the face of newfound liberation.

---

25. For more information concerning the role of women with drums, see Redmond, *When the Drummers Were Women*.

26. Brueggemann, "Exodus," 803.

Dance in Context: Exegesis of Exodus 15:20

In order to understand fully the way Miriam's dance of liberation can revolutionize worship today, it is imperative to look carefully at the text and midrash concerning Miriam's story and dance. This task is difficult because Miriam's narrative occurred during a patriarchal time period; therefore, the meaning of her song and dance is shrouded. Her story was recorded by men seeking to highlight the grandiose attributes and successes of other men. Thus, Miriam's story is often undermined or overshadowed. In the same way that silence gives Miriam birth, much of her life narrative is silenced by the biblical writer.[27]

An interesting aspect of the text that has been misinterpreted for generations deals with the Hebrew word *tof*. Most English translations use the word *tambourine* or *timbrel* to describe the instrument used by Miriam. In addition, most depictions of Miriam in art include a tambourine in her dancing hand. The word tambourine, however, is anachronistic. Carol Meyers, a scholar whose focus emphasizes the history of women in drumming, maintains that there is no evidence that tambourines were invented until the Roman period at the very earliest, and likely not for several more centuries.[28] Rather, the Hebrew word *tof* is literally a handheld frame-drum, which is a hoop-shaped drum with a diameter wider than its depth. This type of drum was quite popular in the ancient Near East and, according to Meyers, "the elements of drum, dance, and song constitute a women's performance genre: the musical celebration of military victory . . . this performance genre was part of the general culture of the eastern Mediterranean in biblical times.[29]

Archaeological evidence supports Meyers' contention. Egyptian wall paintings, scenes on metal and ivory vessels from Cyprus and Phoenicia, as well Mesopotamia, and, most notably small terra-cotta figurines from many Near Eastern sites all depict musicians playing a significant repertoire of musical instruments.[30] In virtually every instance, the frame-drum players are all women and the word for drum players is "unambiguously feminine."[31]

27. Trible, "Bringing Miriam Out of the Shadows," 18.
28. Meyers, "Women with Hand-Drums Dancing," 190.
29. Ibid.
30. Ibid.
31. Ibid.

The second item worth mentioning in the text of Exodus 15:20 is the phrase "went forth." The women "went forth" after Miriam with hand-drums and dancing. Since women typically were limited to the domestic realm, they remained either indoors or within the family compound. Using such a phrase was typical in describing the women who exited their homes to greet husbands, fathers, or sons upon the return from battle. According to Propp, however, in Exodus the phrase is "*pro forma*, since the women were already outside. The sense rather is something like "stepped forward."[32]

Also, according to Iris Stewart, this phrase indicates that Miriam's dance was religious or ritualistic in nature. She contends that, "the phrase 'the women went out after her' tells us it was a female rite, possibly one they learned from the Egyptian priestesses in the temple of Isis."[33] Furthermore, Rabbi Lynn Gottlieb confirms this was the inauguration of a female rite because the word *mahol* in this story, meaning "round dance," appears only as a women's dance.[34] *Mahol* is particularly associated with women.

Also worth mentioning is the shape of Miriam's song in Exodus.[35] The song Miriam chants repeats with variations of the first stanza of the long poem (Exod 15:1–18), earlier attributed to Moses. Such repetition suggests that her contribution is merely derivative and his original. It is as though Moses can sing an entire song, but she can only cite, and then not perfectly, the first stanza.[36] By comparison, her performance appears deficient or less than that of Moses, as does this entire small unit that awkwardly follows the grand Mosaic ending. The song of Moses rambles on and on in grand detail, while Miriam's pithy verse appears to be a second closure, a double ending. "It is anticlimactic, no more an afterthought, a token of the female presence."[37] But it is clear that the very retention of a Miriamic ending in the "presence of a Mosaic avalanche, argues both for its antiquity and authority."[38] So tenacious was the tradition about Miriam that later editors could not eliminate it altogether. Phyllis Trible writes, "In fact, once upon an early time, before editors got jobs, the entire Song of the Sea, not just the first stanza, was ascribed to Miriam and the women of Israel. Later,

32. Propp, *Exodus 1–18*, 547.

33. Stewart, *Sacred Woman, Sacred Dance*, 61.

34. Ibid.

35. All information in this section that references Miriam's song is derived from Trible's research in "Bringing Miriam Out of the Shadows."

36. Trible, "Bringing Miriam Out of the Shadows."

37. Ibid, 19.

38. Ibid.

redactors who were intent upon elevating Moses took the song right out of her mouth and gave it to him."[39]

So, it is clear that Miriam's dance embodied a female rite, as well as offering female leadership for coed worship. Additionally, though the entire song of the sea is often attributed to Moses, the chances are quite likely that it was originally Miriam's song. Or at the very least, it was a song they sang together while dancing on the shores of liberation. This historical context is key if we are to consequently revolutionize our own worship by embodying Miriam's liberating and celebratory dance.

A second way in which to place Miriam's dance in context is to examine various midrashic materials that address her story. The beginning of Miriam's life, as told by midrashic stories, perceptively portrays her character and foreshadows her role as a dancer and leader in her adulthood. In midrash, we discover that when Pharaoh pronounces that all baby boys are to be killed, Miriam's parents divorce in order to avoid the temptation to have more children. Indignant, a young Miriam confronts her parents and scolds them for being worse than Pharaoh. Since Pharaoh had ordered that the boys be killed, Miriam argues that her parents are willing to deny life to girls as well as boys by their choice to divorce. At a young age, Miriam "already earns her name 'rebellious waters' and her parents choose to re-marry and birth Moses."[40] Even as a child, Miriam begins to show signs of the courageous woman she would become.

Pertinent to the study at hand is a midrashic story entitled, "Miriam Under the Mountain."[41] In the hollow of a mountain Miriam discovers an ancient woman. "What is this place?" Miriam asked. "You are in the hollow of the mountain," the old woman said. "Inside the words. The stone tablets that your brother will receive—if he broke them open, this is what he would find. The Torah is the shadow and shell of this place." Miriam trembled. "How am I worthy to have come here?" she asked. "You who tend the wombs of Israel are worthy to tend the womb of Torah," said the old woman. She smiled a sweet smile at Miriam. "Now you will bring back my gifts to the people, just as your brother will bring back gifts."

Puzzled, Miriam wondered if she should take such a gift. "Do you reject my gifts?" asked the old woman sternly. "What have you given me?" Miriam cried. "Empty spaces," said the woman with hair white as lightning.

---

39. Ibid.

40 All details of this midrash come from Mirkin, *The Women Who Danced*, 114.

41. The midrashic story of "Miriam Under the Mountain" is found in Hammer's *Sisters at Sinai*, 131–33.

"Empty spaces?" asked Miriam, confused.

"I have given you all the empty places in the Torah," said the old woman. "Every place there is no ink, every place there is no word, I give to you as my gift."

"That is no great gift," said Miriam.

"Consider," said the woman to Miriam. "Of what is a river made?"

"Water," Miriam answered.

"You are wrong," said the old woman. "A river is an empty channel. Without this hollow, the water would have nowhere to flow. And when the form of this hollow changes, the river changes and becomes a new shape. Now tell me: Of what is your tambourine made?"

"Of silver and wood and skin," Miriam answered. "I know, for I made it myself."

"Again you are wrong," said the old woman. "It is made of emptiness. Without the hollow in its throat, the skin would not chant and the silver would not chime. When you put more or less space between the instrument and your hand, does not its sound change?"

Miriam nodded. "And if you were to ask me of what a dance is made?"

"Yes?" said the old woman.

"I would tell you that it is made of spaces."

"When the world was created," the old woman told Miriam, "it began with space."

In the silent space where the paradoxical presence of freedom and oppression were imminent, Miriam danced. In the muddy space between the waters of the sea, Miriam sang. Miriam's midrash is a reminder of the vital importance of her presence, her dance, and her song.

Miriam's Dance as a Contribution to Israelite Dance

The evidence is clear that Miriam danced as she led the Israelites in liberating praise. However, Miriam's contribution does not end with leaps by the Sea of Reeds. Rather, Miriam's story and dance continued as it had a vital influence on Israelite women and dance. Her lingering truth is found, according to *The Five Books of Miriam,*

> amongst the Daughters of Miriam, the Keepers of the Well, an uninterrupted line of Jewish women who have safeguarded the secret of the Well throughout the generations. And together with this secret, they have gathered up and safeguarded many legends about Miriam and the other ancient mothers of Israel, lovingly

telling and retelling them, mother to daughter, aunt to niece. For legends are fragile things. They need tending to survive the ravages of time. Otherwise they slowly wither away. And the world is poorer for it.[42]

By listening to the legends about Miriam and examining history and archaeology, one may discover the powerful and influential role of Miriam and her dance of liberation.

As Miriam twirled, leapt, and sang in the grips of joy, she joined a tradition that is deeper and grander than her. She became a part of the many women in Scripture who danced. Miriam's dance belongs to a corpus of women's traditions that include the Songs of Deborah (Judg 5:1–31) and Hannah (1 Sam 2:1–10).[43] As the inaugurator of a liberation ritual of songs, drums, and dances in Israel, Miriam continues to resonate throughout its musical life.[44] One can only imagine women of later generations playing hand-drums and dancing as Miriam did, celebrating freedom.

Perhaps Miriam's dance of liberation also paved the way for women to take greater roles in public religious celebrations and rituals. As she led both women and men in song and dance, she was both a prophet and leader. The claim that women were not a part of Israelite leadership must be challenged in light of the stirring evidence of Miriam's song, dance, and leadership on the shores of the Sea of Reeds. According to Meyers, as this custom continued and expanded, surely the opportunity for women to gather to "rehearse, compose, and perform provided women with the opportunity to experience leadership and camaraderie, as well as the esteem of their colleagues."[45] Such an experience would be quite empowering and liberating for women.

While most focus on the exodus as the escape of the Israelites from captivity, with pursuing armies and new lands, the story also includes a recounting of an important women's dance ritual.[46] Miriam's dance was, according to Iris Stewart, an essential and indispensable part of the "festival commemorating the exodus and became one of the climactic ceremonies of the ancient Hebrew Passover festival, *Pesach* or *Pasah*, called the *Hagg*

---

42. Frankel, *The Five Books of Miriam*, xviii.

43. Trible, "Miriam 1," 128.

44. Ibid.

45. Meyers, "Women With Hand-Drums Dancing," 190.

46. Stewart, *Sacred Woman Sacred Dance*, 60–61.

Mazzoth, sacred dance of the pilgrim."[47] The purpose of this festival or dance was letting go of and forgetting a troubled past, a ritual also associated with the Midianites or Kenites, who worshiped the Great Mother in the copper mines of Sinai.[48]

In Hebrew tradition it is also prophesied that at the "great banquet time of the Messiah, Miriam will dance before the righteous."[49] It is evident that Miriam's dance played a tremendous role in women's dances in ancient Israel. She provided pathways for leadership and the enduring hope of liberation from bondage. Traces of Miriam's dance must have crept into the choreography of little girls as they played. Every time the women gathered to dance at festivals, Miriam's example probably guided their steps as they remembered their liberation and the woman who danced to celebrate it.

How Miriam's Dance Can Revolutionize Worship Today

The character of Miriam and her liberating dance provide a myriad of glimpses into the lives of ancient Israelites: what they held as sacred, to what they ascribed value, and most notably, the manner in which they embodied their worship. Her legacy lives on, despite the minimal space she is given in Scripture. Not only did Miriam's dance create pathways for other women in biblical times, it also provides inspiration for countless artists and dancers in our modern world, and offers us liberating fodder for worship today.

Miriam's dance is the classic example of joyful and liberating dance in worship. Celebratory processionals, joyful high holy days, and simple upbeat choreography with drums and rhythm instruments are ideal examples of how to portray Miriam's dance. Something as simple as having the choir and clergy process in while swaying with rhythm instrument, singing a song about liberation and freedom would be powerful. Utilizing the liberating power of spirituals, such as "Swing Low, Sweet Chariot," "Woke Up This Mornin' With My Mind Stayed on Freedom," or "Wade in the Water" would parallel both the water and dance imagery embedded in the text. Getting the entire congregation involved in the movement by processing in or out of the worship space would also recall the liberating power of the exodus event, especially if jars of water, rhythm instruments, and drums were passed throughout the congregation while singing and dancing up or down the aisles.

47. Ibid., 61.
48. Ibid.
49. Ibid.

In more performative categories, several popular dancers have creative evocative choreography featuring Miriam's dance. *Miriam, Sister of Moses*[50] was produced in California in 1919 as a full-length play with dance; Miriam was played by Ruth St. Denis, with Ted Shawn creating the choreography. Long sweeping movements across the stage describe much of this choreography, illustrating, perhaps, a journey from bondage to freedom. Other examples of choreography inspired by Miriam's dance include Loie Fuller's creation of *Miriam's Dance* in 1911, which depicts the story of leaving the bondage of Egypt and crossing the Sea of Reeds. Also, the famous dancer Rachel Nadav played Miriam the Prophetess.[51] In 1944 the prima ballerina Anna Sokolow created a series of dances on biblical women including Sarah and Miriam that was called *Song of a Semite*. Martha Graham, however, is the choreographer best known for creating choreography about biblical women that did not limit women's roles to evil seductresses but instead depicted dynamic and deep characters. Utilizing the gifts of a dancer within the congregation with training in modern dance or ballet would be the perfect opportunity to highlight Miriam's liberating dance as choreographed by some of the aforementioned dancers.

Reading the story of Miriam in worship, preaching about her dance, singing hymns and songs that reflect the power of her liberating dance, and weaving liberation theology into dance, preaching, visual art, music, and poetry are all vital was to help revolutionize worship today. Liberation is not only at the heart of Miriam's dance, it is also the heart of the gospel. For worship to reflect such good news, it must also embody liberation in real and tangible ways. Processionals, rhythm instruments, and dances each offer the opportunity to reflect on the imperative role of joyful liberation in worship.

Miriam, this liberating dancer and prophetess, was clearly part of the triumvirate of leadership with Moses and Aaron, and was responsible for guiding the people from slavery into liberty. So, too, may she lead us to liberation. Her dance created pathways toward freedom for women leading in ritual and worship. Her song provided hope in the midst of despair. So, too, must our songs and dances. If we truly want to revolutionize worship, it must liberate all people so that everyone may join Miriam on the shores freedom.

---

50. All information concerning the play *Miriam, Sister of Moses* is found in Manor's *The Gospel According to Dance*, 17–18.

51. Manor, *Gospel According to Dance*, 123.

CHAPTER 3

Jephthah's Daughter's Dance: Lamentation
Judges 11:34

From the tyranny of the vow,
from the blood of the sacrifice,
the unnamed child turned not back,
the courage of the daughter turned not away . . .

Ye daughters of Israel, weep for your sister,
who suffered the betrayal of her foolish father,
who turned to you for solace and love.

How are the powerless fallen,
a terrible sacrifice to a faithless vow!

—PHYLLIS TRIBLE[1]

The story of Jephthah's daughter remains enigmatic and disturbing to contemporary readers. The tale of this nameless young child, with scarcely a voice of her own and with her violent fate precipitated and carried out by her own father, is surely "one of the most horrifying tales in the whole Bible."[2] For generations the question of what really happened to Jephthah's daughter has preoccupied biblical scholars. The "sacrificialists" have argued that Jephthah kept his vow, literally, while the "nonsacrificialists"

---

1. Trible, *Texts of Terror*, 109.
2. Bohmbach, "Daughter of Jephthah," 244.

have argued that Jephthah let his daughter survive.[3] Other scholars, such as Esther Fuchs, believe it is precisely the ambiguity that characterizes the description of the sacrifice that is typical of the entire story. Fuchs proposes that the ambiguity functions as a type of apology, a subtle justification of Jephthah's behavior. By neglecting to share details about the sacrifice, the narrator makes it possible for readers to forget that the sacrifice has ever taken place. Fuchs states that though, "the tragedy is ultimately the daughter's, it is Jephthah who is presented as the tragic victim of circumstances. The daughter is sacrificed in more than one sense in our story, for the center of attention continues to be Jephthah."[4]

For reasons such as these, it is difficult to understand the character of Jephthah's daughter; her voice is practically unheard and her dance is given scarcely a sentence in the biblical narrative. The story is told from Jephthah's point of view, both perceptually and emotionally. By using ambiguity at key points, the writer of the text leaves to conjecture actions whose detailed descriptions might have condemned the father. However, the purpose of this chapter is to discover the purpose and role of, not Jephthah's actions, but Jephthah's daughter's actions, namely her dance. What role did Jephthah's daughter's dance have in her violent fate? How did dance function in the lamentation of the Israelite women after her sacrifice? How can dance function liturgically in lamentation today?

The story of this unnamed dancer appears near the end of her father's story. Its position, as well as the events that it narrates, suggest that it functions primarily as a further explanation of the character of her father.[5] Sadly, Scriptures and the history of the church have, according to Trible, "failed to perceive and interpret the nuances of this story. For centuries, patriarchal hermeneutics has forgotten the daughter of Jephthah but remembered her father, indeed exalted him."[6] More ink is shed over the particularity of Jephthah's sacrifice than over the description of his daughter's dance. As in much of history, the mighty warrior prevails uncensored; the violence that he perpetuated on his only child—his dancing daughter—haunts him very little.

Jephthah's daughter is nameless in the text. And she is merely a child. Since the text tells us that she is a virgin, one can deduce that she had not

---

3. Fuchs, "Marginalization, Ambiguity, Silencing," 35.
4. Ibid.
5. Bohmbach, "Daughter of Jephthah," 243.
6. Trible, *Texts of Terror*, 107.

yet reached puberty, since women typically married at that time. Her dance was characterized by the joy of a child who celebrates the return of her father from his travels. However, Jephthah's daughter sees post-victory celebration evolve into lamentation. Jumps and twirls of greeting, jubilation, and welcome-home evolve into a dance of lamentation for a life short-lived as Jephthah's nameless daughter succumbs to the foolish promise of her faithless father.

The Daughter

Jephthah's daughter is not the focus of the narrative in Judges 11; rather she is an interruption. What brings Jephthah's daughter onto the stage of our story is an accident—her unpredictable emergence from her father's house. Her dance of greeting establishes the fundamental rules that will undergird the daughter's presentation henceforth. She is nameless; she is identified and defined only by her relationship with Jephthah; she is an only daughter deemed unworthy of a name or any details describing her; it is this father-daughter relationship that underlies her characterization and determines her significance in the story.[7] So, what *do* we know about this nameless daughter? We know that she is Jephthah's only daughter, that she dances, and that she is a virgin. In fact, her virginity is mentioned three times during the narrative. Virginity functions much like beauty in women as a mark of high distinction, a symbol of their worth. The emphasis on the daughter's virginity implies that she has not yet produced children, and therefore, the loss of Jephthah's genealogy. Like the note on her being an only child, the emphasis on her virginity indicates what her loss means to Jephthah. It tells us little about her. Furthermore, the mention of her virginity indicates that she was most likely a young child and was still considered Jephthah's property. Her death would indicate the loss of one of Jephthah's major assets. According to Fuchs, "that the daughter is Jephthah's only child tells us more about her importance for *him* than about her. A minor character, her significance to the story derives from her relationship with her father."[8]

While she is a minor character, what is ostensible in the biblical text is that Jephthah's daughter is obedient to her father's wishes. This obedience is illustrated primarily in her response to her father once she discovers that she is the victim of his vow. While she may be unaware that her physical life

7. Fuchs, "Marginalization, Ambiguity, Silencing," 37.
8. Ibid.

is at stake, she is quickly willing to obey her father. In these ways, Jephthah's is the "supreme image of the perfect daughter, whose loyalty and submissiveness to her father knows no limits."[9] Therefore, the text does not portray a tragically faithful and obedient servant of Yahweh, but of her father.

Had she challenged her father, Jephthah's daughter would be implicitly challenging Yahweh's authority as well, for Jephthah's vow was made to God, and she is the means of realizing it. Thus, the daughter's calm response and subsequent silence permit the reader to remain focused on the father's grief instead of hers. If Jephthah's daughter had begged for mercy, had she asked to be spared, had she turned to Yahweh with a plea for absolution or exception, the reader would grieve too much for her, so much so that Jephthah's refusal to grant her freedom would have cast both him and Yahweh in a negative light.

The text describes Jephthah rending his clothing upon witnessing his daughter's dance. However, Jephthah does not rend his garments in a traditional gesture of mourning but indicates that his grief is for himself as the victim of a foolish vow and not for the real victim. By contrast, the daughter is the epitome of faithfulness. Her actions reveal her as one who is loyal to the standards of her covenant community. Trible contends further:

> Faithfulness to an unfaithful vow has condemned its victim; father and daughter are split apart in deed and destiny. Though in anguish he calls her "my daughter," he offers her neither solace nor release . . . Although his daughter has served him devotedly with music and dance, Jephthah bewails the calamity that she brings upon him. *And throughout it all God says nothing* . . . She [the daughter] does not seek to deny or defy them, nor does she show anger or depression. No sentiment or self-pity passes her lips; instead, she feels for her father the compassion that he has not extended to her.[10]

Scholars ask: Where is God in this terrifying tale? Questions of theodicy abound as some theologians feel that Jephthah cannot bear the blame alone but that his daughter is also guilty in her tragic fate. Esther Fuchs states, "to the extent that the daughter's greetings are the effect of her independent initiative she too is responsible for her own death . . . To some extent, the daughter actively participates in the process leading to her own demise."[11]

---

9. Ibid., 42–43.

10. Trible, *Texts of Terror*, 102 (italics mine).

11. Fuchs, "Marginalization, Ambiguity, Silencing," 39.

For Fuchs, the daughter's death is the product of a collaborative effort on the part of herself and her father. Although the narrative seeks to demonstrate the fatal mistake of Jephthah as judge and leader and his tragedy as father, it does not describe the way he brutally sacrificed his daughter because a father is never shown to be the direct perpetrator of his daughter's death.[12] Rather Jephthah is shown as a helpless victim of unforeseen circumstances, "caught in the web of conflicting allegiances, and insurmountable constraints."[13]

It is also interesting to compare this story with the story found in Genesis 22. Trible reminds us how very different the narrative of Jephthah's daughter is compared to the story of Abraham's near sacrifice of Isaac.[14] In the case of the only son, detailed descriptions abound and the narrative builds suspense as the reader waits for the moment when Isaac is sacrificed. But we can bear these details because we know that Isaac is not sacrificed. He is spared. In the tale of the dancing daughter, no angel intervenes. No ram appears. The father carries out the human vow precisely as he spoke it; neither God nor man nor woman negates it. "Accordingly, the narrator spares us the suspense and agony of details; the despicable outcome is sufficient unto itself . . . Though the son is saved, the daughter is slain . . . A vow led to victory; victory produced a victim; the victim died by violence; violence has, in turn, fulfilled the vow."[15] The faithless vow prevails, and in its presence even the deity to whom it was addressed remains silent.

Trible writes: "Under the power of the vow, the daughter has breathed her last. My God, my God, why hast though forsaken her?"[16] In comparing the two pericopes, one notices that Jephthah is not Abraham; Abraham is described as faithful, whereas Jephthah is not. Furthermore, the son of promise had a name: Isaac. He also had a respectable family lineage: a mother named Sarai and a grandfather named Terah. By contrast, the daughter of the mighty warrior Jephthah is nameless. "Her father is of illegitimate birth; her mother is never mentioned; her grandmother was a harlot; her grandfather cannot be identified. So the girl emerges as an isolated figure in the tradition of Israel as well as in this particular story."[17] The

---

12. Ibid.

13. Ibid.

14. Trible, *Texts of Terror*, 105.

15. Ibid.

16. Ibid.

17. Ibid.

text describes her as his one and only child; besides her he had neither son nor daughter. Isaac, too, was an only child. But the promised son, Isaac, will live, while the nameless daughter must die.

As a potential mother, the daughter represents the future for family and community, the legacy of Jephthah's name. His daughter may be remembered by few, but how can she be mourned for properly when readers and hearers do not even know her name? According to Ackerman, "Jephthah's daughter is lauded in Judges' Deuteronomistic prose for her act of religious piety and, moreover, the ways in which she manifests this piety as opposed to the faithlessness exhibited by the man in her life."[18] But, for all the religious authority that Judges 11 ascribes to Jephthah's daughter, the tradition does not bother to give her a name. On the other hand, the meaning of Jephthah's name carries tremendous weight as it means "God opens the womb," although the act of Jephthah opening his mouth surely closed the womb of his virgin daughter.

The Role of a Dancing Daughter

The specific role and function of a daughter who dances is never mentioned in the Hebrew Bible, nor is any concrete evidence found in extracanonical material. There is ample indication regarding women exiting their homes to greet victors with a dance of victory or greeting, as Jephthah's daughter did. That the daughter greeted her father with dance was not unusual; the aspect that is out of the ordinary is the father's vow. The father and the community are aware of the vow; the only one who is unaware of the ironic incongruity is the daughter. Greeting her father with hand-drums and dance the daughter is presented as a victim of dramatic irony; she does not yet know the fateful meaning of her joyful actions.[19] The incompatibility of her joy and Jephthah's grief further "intensifies the incongruity between her limited knowledge and reality."[20]

Also, the text offers more description of Jephthah's actions than of his daughter's, with little description of her dance: "Whereas in Jephthah's case, the text dramatizes the gestures and words of the grief-stricken father, in the daughter's case it contents itself with a summary description: 'and she departed, she and her female friends, and lamented her virginity upon the

18. Ackerman, *Warrior, Dancer, Seductress, Queen*, 115.
19. Fuchs, "Marginalization, Ambiguity, Silencing," 38.
20. Ibid.

mountain.' How Jephthah's daughter mourns and laments is not specified. Again, greater specificity at this point might have generated too much sympathy for the daughter."[21] In making his vow, did Jephthah not know that it was customary in Israel for women to come out and greet victorious male warriors with song and dance upon their return from battle and that it is quite likely that his daughter would also follow this custom?

Another question concerns whether Jephthah's daughter had prior knowledge of her father's vow before she dances out of the house. The text suggests that Jephthah's vow was made in their hometown of Mizpah; if pronounced publicly, presumably she would have heard it. However, the ambiguity of Jephthah's vow disappears. His daughter *is* his sacrifice; she must die for his unfaithfulness.

To those acquainted with the traditions of her people, her appearance and activity is no surprise. Women danced after David's return from battle (1 Sam 18:6–7), Miriam danced after crossing the Sea of Reeds (Exod 15:20), and countless other women danced with greeting, victory, and lamentation. Jephthah's daughter is part of such ancient company. Like the women before her—and possibly throughout her community on that same day—she danced out "with timbrels and dances" to meet her victorious father. Unlike them, she comes alone, and no words of a song appear on her lips.[22] This notable difference accents the terrible irony of an otherwise typical and joyful occasion.

It is not difficult to imagine Jephthah's daughter similar to young, dancing daughters of today, carefully and playfully choreographing routines for the return of their traveling fathers. As this young child danced through the doorway, mindfully recalling her choreographed steps, prepared for the return of her father, she did not know that her actions would "bring him low" (Judg 11:35). The thoughtful and playful role of a dancing daughter, therefore, is overshadowed by the foolishness of her father. Her well-planned routines are replaced by the rending of garments and lamentation for the loss of a possible lineage. Today we rend our garments for this dancing daughter and lament for the loss of her name.

After Jephthah's daughter dances out her doorway to greet her father, and realizes that she shall become the victim of his vow, she requests that he let her alone for two months. But then she adds, "I and my female friends" (Judg 11:37). At a time of deepest sorrow, the last days of her life, the girl

21. Ibid., 43.
22. Ibid.

reaches out to other women, not her father or family. She chooses these women to go with her to wander upon the hills and lament her virginity. "In communion with her own kind, she transcends the distance between daughter and father."[23] After this, Jephthah's daughter speaks no more. In the company of other women who acknowledge her tragedy, she is neither alone nor isolated. In this company, she begins an ancient custom. According to Ackerman, "Jephthah's daughter is one of the women who play a decisive role in ancient Israelite cultic matters . . . these portrayals are possible because they stem from the period of religious instability associated with the composition of the Deuteronomistic History."[24] The fact that a tradition begins because of human activity is almost as remarkable as the notion that it begins because of the actions of a female child. Throughout the biblical tradition, annual ritual events occur on Israel's behalf because of the actions of Yahweh, with human activity commemorating a ritual on a rare occasion. "For most of Israel's history, the ritual founded by Jephthah's daughter stands alone as an observance that commemorates a human character and her deeds . . . It is equally extraordinary that the ritual Jephthah's daughter founds is a *women's* ritual, for the Bible in general tells us very little about the nature of women's religious lives."[25] And so the women gather annually to dance and lament—silent protests amidst the screams of patriarchy and violence.

As certain ritual practices in ancient Israel, as in many cultures, are related to men, so too are some the prerogative of women. In fact, due to the androcentric culture of her time, few references are given to women's rituals in the Hebrew Bible; in these ways, Jephthah's daughter stands alone as the inaugurator of such a feminist rite.[26] The details of the commemorative practice are not given, but the fact that these young women "go out" to carry out this custom indicates that it was not likely done in a domestic setting, but in the mountains and in the community of women from outside of the household. Like the dance of lamentation and wailing after the daughter's death, the commemorative mourning is particularly suitable for an annual female custom, given the fact that women, rather than men, tended to be specialists in funerary practices in ancient Israel. Meyers additionally contends that "this custom also provides an exegetical

---

23. Ibid., 104.

24. Ackerman, *Warrior, Dancer, Seductress, Queen*, 109.

25. Ibid., 111.

26. Meyers et al., *Women in Scripture*, 244.

example of female bonding; the dynamics of a single-gender gathering that lasted for four days inevitably would have fostered extensive interaction, shared experience, and a sense of connection."[27] It has been suggested that the women's mourning rite subsequently became regularized in Israelite society—that is, it came to be a custom for young women to go out annually together. Some have suggested that this custom functioned as a rite of passage, a ritual recognition of the crossover from childhood to adulthood.[28] For many women this ritual would illustrate their readiness for marriage. Accordingly, Jephthah's daughter is at an even deeper loss because after such ritual she cannot join her beloved female community in marriage preparations.

Amidst the accolades of her contribution to Israelite dance via her annual lamentation ritual, Jephthah's daughter's dance is still delineated by the patriarchal overshadowing found in the Judges narrative. By tagging on a postscript about the annual mourning of Jephthah's daughter, Fuchs suggests that the "narrator would counterbalance the daughter's horrid end. Literary strategies work here in the interests of patriarchal ideology, the ideology of male supremacy."[29] That it became a custom for Israelite women to mourn four days a year shifts our focus from the daughter to the annual custom. Androcentrism prevails as the narrator fails to include any information about the ritual event the daughter founds and silences its female participants by denying the importance of their religious expression. Nonetheless, according to Phyllis Trible,

> Death and silence are not, however, the final words of the story . . . "She became a tradition in Israel." Whereas the female who has never known a man is typically numbered among the unremembered, in the case of the daughter of Jephthah the usual does not happen. Although *she* had not known a man, nevertheless, *she* became a tradition in Israel. In a dramatic way this sentence alters, though it does not eliminate, the finality of Jephthah's faithless vow. The alteration comes through the faithfulness of the women of Israel . . . The unnamed virgin child becomes a tradition in Israel because the women with whom she chose to spend her last days have not let her pass into oblivion . . . The narrative postscript,

---

27. Ibid., 245.

28. Bohmbech, "Companions of Jephthah's Daughter," 245.

29. Fuchs, "Marginalization, Ambiguity, Silencing," 45.

then, shifts the focus of the story from vow to victim, from death to life, from oblivion to remembrance.[30]

Jephthah's daughter's role may be overshadowed, but her ritual will be remembered forever. The women of Israel will not allow her voice to go unheard as they dance to remember the tragedy of Jephthah's daughter. In the same way that ancient Israelite women mourned her death, so too must women today. How did Jephthah's daughter's dance contribute to Israelite dance? It provided Israelite women with an opportunity to lament all the women who had been forsaken. Her dance of greeting paved the way for other oppressed women to embody their lamentation through a custom that is ritualized year after year. Jephthah's daughter stands alone as the only human in the Hebrew Bible to initiate such as legacy.

Jephthah's Daughter's Dance in Context

Then Jephthah came to his home at Mizpah; and there was his daughter coming out to meet him with hand drums and with dancing. She was his only child; he had no son or daughter except her.[31]

It is clear that a character analysis of Jephthah's daughter is important in understanding her dance. Also imperative to the study is placing her dance in context. Plucking Jephthah's daughter's dance out of its historical context does little for those seeking to understand her role in ancient Israelite dance, or how her dance might inform our worship today. Therefore, it is vital to examine Judges 11:34 and place the narrative in its literary context in order to understand more completely Jephthah's daughter's dance.

The narrative of Jephthah's sacrifice of his one and only daughter spans six compact verses (Judg 11:34–40) which are embedded in a larger interlude that disrupts the flow of two success stories: Jephthah's victory over the Ammonites (Judg 11:33) and his conquest of the Ephraimites (Judg 12:4).[32] Details regarding his daughter's dance or the subsequent ritual of lamentation performed annually by Israelite women are lacking. However, noteworthy are Jephthah's words of response to his daughter's dance and the ambiguity of the results of his faithless vow.

30. Trible, *Texts of Terror*, 106–7.

31. Judges 11:34. Translation mine.

32. Fuchs, "Marginalization, Ambiguity, Silencing," 36.

The words, "you have brought me to my knees" and "you have been among my enemies" (Judg11:35) are a selfish accusation on Jephthah's behalf. Instead of considering his daughter's fate, Jephthah essentially accuses her of working in partnership with his enemies.[33] Jephthah's focus, in word and deed, is on himself, not on his daughter or her possible fate. When the daughter dances out of her father's door, the text does not explain what the daughter knows. The reader is left to surmise that Jephthah tells his daughter about his vow, but the details are missing. How much she knows is unclear, namely how and when she will be sacrificed. In these ways, the narrator avoids any explicitness that might indict Jephthah or generate too much sympathy for his daughter.[34]

The absence of a clear reference to the daughter's prospective sacrifice or, retroactively to Jephthah's vow, cannot be explained merely by the fact that the text has already referred to it previously. Fuchs contends that "repetition is a hallmark of biblical prose, just as informational omissions are; it is valid to question both phenomena whenever they occur."[35] Phyllis Trible notes that the ambiguity of the sacrifice is indicative of its finality:

> The nature of the sacrifice is, however, as unclear as it is emphatic. Literally, the words read, "the comer-forth who comes forth," a compound expression of emphasis that is difficult to render in English. Moreover, the masculine gender of these terms is a standard grammatical usage that by itself does not identify either species or sex. A certain vagueness lurks in these words of Jephthah, and we do well to let it be. Did he intend a human sacrifice, male or female? A servant perhaps? Or an animal?[36]

The story fails to clarify the precise meaning of his words; we shall know it by the fruits. In linking Jephthah's private life with a public crisis, the savior figure has spoken on his own, for neither Yahweh nor the people of Gilead require the vow. The Israelites never ordain child-sacrifice; this is a Canaanite practice specifically condemned by Israelite law according to Leviticus.[37] Furthermore, Jephthah's vow has disrupted the flow of the narrated discourse. It has broken in at the very center to plead for divine help that is already Jephthah's through the spirit of Yahweh. It appears that

33. Ibid., 39.
34. Ibid., 40–41.
35. Ibid., 41.
36. Trible, *Texts of Terror*, 96–97.
37. Hamlin, *Judges*, 118.

Jephthah desires to bind God rather than embrace the gift of the spirit. The precise consequences of Jephthah's vow are unclear, but the recipient of oppression is, indeed, his daughter. In these ways, careful exegesis of the narrative surrounding Jephthah's daughter's dance is important, as is examining the literary context.

Literary Context of Jephthah's Daughter's Dance

Esther Fuchs suggests that, rather than taking the story of Jephthah's daughter as a reflection of historical reality, we should consider it as an ideological construction. She suggests that the construction of the narrative's much-discussed ambiguity understates the father's culpability at the expense of his daughter.[38] The ambiguity of the sacrifice stands as a paradigm for the rest of the narrative. The daughter's joyous greeting follows her father's victory just as later on her mourning will follow both temporally and etiologically her father's grievous outburst. Thus the verse introducing the daughter depicts her most important characteristic—that is her complete obedience to her father—a most welcome characteristic from a patriarchal point of view.

Phyllis Trible suggests that the narrative of Judges 11 can be divided into two tragic episodes: "slaughter in episode one begets sacrifice in episode two . . . Episode one involves a public slaughter and episode two, a private sacrifice."[39] The private sacrifice leads to a time of mourning:

> That time is to be filled with lamentation, not for death, but for unfulfilled life . . . First, it is premature; life ends before its potential has unfolded . . . Second, her death is to be violent. Death by fire is bitter death, and more bitter still when its author is her very own father. Third, her death will leave no heirs because she is a virgin. What alone designated fulfillment for every Hebrew woman, the bearing of children, will never be hers to know . . . she may be numbered among the unremembered . . . Hers is premeditated death, a sentence of murder passed upon an innocent victim because of the faithless vow uttered by her foolish father.[40]

Amidst the terror of this child-sacrifice, one wonders why no one, not even Yahweh, intervenes. In the narrative of Abraham's near-sacrifice of his son, Isaac, Yahweh sends an angel to prevent the killing. That sacrifice, however,

---

38. Fuchs, "Marginalization, Ambiguity, Silencing," 36.

39. Trible, *Texts of Terror*, 93.

40. Ibid., 104.

was God's idea in the first place. Even though Israelites do not permit child sacrifice, no one intervenes or demands that Jephthah not fulfill his vow. Why do the women friends of the daughter not intervene, convincing her to run away and so escape her fate? And where is the daughter's mother?[41] If repetition and omission are, indeed, the hallmarks of biblical prose, then the omission of Jephthah's wife is worth mentioning. Is her voice missing because of patriarchal writers, or did she support Jephthah's vow to Yahweh? The literary structure that omits her potential voice is both chilling and telling.

It is indisputably clear that Jephthah's nameless daughter played a tremendous role in the dance of ancient Israel. She instigated a custom of yearly lament and greeted her father with a dance of victory, much like Miriam's dance in Exodus. Even with her death, she becomes an unmistakable symbol for all the courageous daughters of faithless fathers.[42] Her story is obscure in Scripture. Her dance has been forgotten by many. And her name remains unknown. It is now our responsibility to mourn her tragic death, to dance her dance and to rend our garments in the spirit of remembrance.

How Jephthah's Daughter's Dance Revolutionizes Worship Today

In order to understand how the dance of Jephthah's daughter can revolutionize worship today and teach us about the importance of lament, I turn to a story from my own childhood. When I was a little girl, I can remember diligently working on choreography to make up routines to perform for my family. From Tina Turner to "Don't Worry Be Happy" to Michael Jackson's "Beat It" I can remember making up creative routines and performing them in front of the affirming audience that was my family. Often times, my routines were accompanied by props, such as a Hula-Hoop, roller skates, or an unwilling younger brother. Whether I had props or not, there was always a big smile on my face as I twirled and leapt to the tunes on my family's 8-track, record, or cassette player. Half the fun was making up the routine and practicing until it was performance perfect. The other half of the fun was the response on my family's faces as I forced them to "watch me, watch me!" once again. Despite the cheesiness of my routines and my silly props, they watched with delight, clapped, and encouraged me to dance all the more. Such is the experience for many young children throughout

41. Bohmbach, "Companions of Jephthah's Daughter," 243.

42. Trible, *Texts of Terror*, 108.

childhood: choreographing routines, drawing pictures, making up skits and plays, and practicing to make their parents proud.

It is these very aspects of childhood play that haunt the story of Jephthah's daughter found in Judges 11. A little girl skips out of her house to perform her newest routine upon the return of her daddy; little does she know what fate awaits her. Jumps and twirls of greeting, celebration, and welcome-home evolve into a dance of lamentation for a life short-lived as Jephthah's daughter succumbs to the foolish promise of her faithless father.

The story of Jephthah's faithless vow and his dancing daughter's demise stands as a paradigm for so many innocent victims that have suffered at the hands of proud people in power. This young daughter, who is not even awarded a name in Scripture, is quite similar to the many who suffer injustices today. I think of the countless girls who have been victims of violence at the hands of faithless fathers. I think of individuals and families caught in cycles of violence, nameless victims whose stories we never hear. I think of voiceless mothers who witness the deaths of their children to war or gang violence.

Naming such violence and victimization is a first step in acknowledging the need for lament in worship and ritual. Listing or reading the names of children who have been sacrificed at the hands of faithless vows throughout the world provides the potential for healing. So, too, does offering an embodied response to such violence. Too often, dance is placed in the category of rejoicing; lamentation, like Jephthah's daughter's name, is forgotten. As we have seen in the Exodus event, dance can, indeed, express joy and liberation. But the dance is not limited to transcendence, leaps of joy, or twirls of celebration. In the same way that the body aches, ages, and ails, the body can also express lamentation through dance.

Forming a group of dancers and movers to study the story of Jephthah's daughter's dance and then imagine how the women of Israel mourned her death with their bodies would be powerful to share in worship. Experimenting with breath in a time of corporate prayer by expanding and contracting the abdomen and chest in such a way that contractions embody a physical response to pain, suffering, and lamentation is also an embodied possibility. Additionally, if there are trained dancers in the congregation, utilizing the choreography of Martha Graham's *Lamentation* or Alvin Ailey's first movement, "I Been Buked," from *Revelations* would be sure to revitalize worship in a way that gives voice to the deep need for lamentation.

Graham's *Lamentation* involves a solo dancer wrapped in tube of stretchy fabric and begins seated on a bench; each movement looks as though she is trying to escape, to reach out for freedom, as though the tragedy she laments has trapped her body. Open, active, reaching hands describe many of the gestures throughout, as though the hands are wailing, lamenting loss. So, too, are the open hands in Ailey's "I Been Buked," as they grasp for something other than being buked and scorned. Heads tilted back, necks exposed, and chests lifted, the most vulnerable parts of the dancer's body are open and on display, expressing pain, suffering, and lamentation. Imagine partnering the reading of Jephthah's daughter's dance with the choreography of Graham or Ailey.

Yet another opportunity to express lament with the body is to teach simple choreography to children to a song such as Kurt Bestor's "Prayer of the Children." After witnessing the brutality of war while serving as a missionary in Serbia in the 1970s, Bestor penned these lyrics on behalf of the children who suffered as victims of violence:

> *Can you hear the prayer of the children*
> *on bended knee, in the shadow of an unknown room?*
> *Empty eyes with no more tears to cry*
> *turning heavenward toward the light.*
> *Crying, "Jesus, help me*
> *to see the morning light of one more day,*
> *but if I should die before I wake,*
> *I pray my soul to take."*

> *Can you feel the hearts of the children*
> *aching for home, for something of their very own.*
> *Reaching hands with nothing to hold onto*
> *but hope for a better day, a better day.*
> *Crying, "Jesus, help me*
> *to feel the love again in my own land,*
> *but if unknown roads lead away from home,*
> *give me loving arms, away from harm."*

> *Can you hear the voice of the children*
> *softly pleading for silence in their shattered world?*
> *Angry guns preach a gospel full of hate,*
> *blood of the innocent on their hands.*

Crying, "Jesus, help me
to feel the sun again upon my face?
For when darkness clears, I know you're near,
bringing peace again."

Can you hear the prayer of the children?[43]

It is, in fact, children that danced their prayers on behalf of their sacrificed friend, Jephthah's daughter. It is the child who suffered, the daughter who was sacrificed. Giving children the opportunity to express their own lament is an evocative way to teach adults about the importance of embodying their lamentation in worship, as well.

In order for worship to encapsulate the entire Christian experience, lamentation cannot be forgotten. We also must not forget the dance of Jephthah's daughter. In the same way that celebration and liberation must be a part of our embodied worshiping lives, so too must lamentation. The story of Jephthah's daughter provides the perfect transition from celebration to lament, invoking the words from Ecclesiastes: there is a time to mourn and a time dance.[44] In the case of Jephthah's daughter, worship is a time for both.

---

43. See www.kurtbestorsheetmusic.com.

44. Ecclesiastes 3:4. Translation mine.

CHAPTER 4

David's Dance: Abandon

2 Samuel 6:5–23

Gods of ecstasy revel
Bacchanalian debauchery writhes and whirls
Dionysian abandon dances on tabletops
David reveals
God's ultimate rock star

King David is joined by 30,000 others in bringing the ark of the covenant from the House of Obed-Edom. We can probably agree that it's likely that there weren't exactly 30,000 people, but that is no matter. The point is that there were *a lot* of people and that their worship was celebration at its finest. Mind you, worship can be reverent. Worship can express lament. Worship can embody transcendence. But in 2 Samuel, David and the other Israelites were so caught in the grips of God's joy that their worship is best described as celebration.

They had songs. They had lyres. They had harps and tambourines and drums and castanets and cymbals. It was a raucous time. In the midst of it all—between God's glory shining forth from the ark and the pulse of the music—David got caught up in the spirit. 2 Samuel tells us that "David danced before the Lord with all his might." Shouting people. Clanging symbols. Beating drums. Pulsating music. Dionysian abandon. Ecstatic worship. A dancing king. All the words are active. It is as though the Hebrew language in the passage thrusts us forward, our bodies responding with kinesthetic identification as we too become caught up in the celebration.

And then the text pauses with an interesting tidbit of information that is not the slightest bit related to movement or worship or celebration.

It is a precarious description of this dancing king. "David was girded with a linen ephod." We are left scratching our heads, wondering what this odd descriptive detail has to do with King David's worship. And then the action continues. Dancing David, the musicians, the shouting people, and the ark came into the city of David and "Michal, daughter of Saul looked out of the window, and saw King David leaping and dancing before the Lord; and she despised him in her heart" (2 Sam 6:16).

This is where many preachers and scholars jump to swift conclusions and demonize David's wife, Michal, quickly elevating David as God's ultimate rock star and claiming that Michal was too pagan or too prudish or lacked the spirit. Such scholars pay no mind that David was essentially "revealing his glory" to the whole city as he writhes and whirls in his linen ephod. Interestingly, wearing such a revealing garment was prohibited in worship precisely because bowing, prostrating, and dancing were such essential parts of ancient Israelite worship (Exod 20:26). Accordingly, I would like to dedicate the bulk of this chapter to understanding why David danced and Michal despised. Understanding the intent behind these actions is pivotal for grasping how David's dance can revolutionize worship today.

Why David Danced and Michal Despised: Four Theories

While it is impossible to enter the mind of biblical characters and know exactly the intention behind dancing in a particular way or despising in a particular way, it behooves us to examine four theories that may point us toward a greater understanding of the worshipful nuances in 2 Samuel 6. These theories include the traditional, the parody, the sexual, and the communal.

The first and most widely proclaimed theory is what I call the traditional theory. Simply put, this theory notes that ecstatic abandon is the natural result of one who is caught in the grips of God's joy. David was merely dancing out of his deep and unabashed love for God; he was so caught up in the spirit that his clothing, his exposure, his public display mattered not. Michal, according to this traditional view, lacked the spirit. Her place is in the home and she wrongly asserts herself by stepping into the public sphere and speaking against David's worshipful abandon. Michal is jealous of David because she believes her father, Saul, should be king.

Further, she views David's dance as a public spectacle that undermines the traditional understanding of what it means to be king. According to the traditional view, Michal lacks the spirit. She is jealous. She is a nagging wife. And she could never imagine worshiping with as much abandon as her faithful husband.

The *Geneva Notes* state that the reason Michal is barren is because she mocks the servant of God (David). Matthew Henry's commentary describes Michal as peevish and proud, noting that she was embarrassed at David's lack of decorum. While admonishing David's abandon as he dances with all his might, traditionalists are quick to condemn Michal. For example, Henry denounces her behavior, saying, "She unjustly reproached David for his devotion, and therefore God justly put her under the perpetual reproach of barrenness."[1] Edith Deen calls Michal "not at all religious" and claims she has the unbridled tongue of James when she states "Michal's sharp tongue set in motion the sudden end of what had been a good marriage. Michal was the real loser. She lost a good home, a husband, who became Israel's greatest king, and the love of the people over whom her husband ruled."[2] In other words, traditionalists believe that David is good and Michal is bad. They are opposites without complexity or nuance. I would surmise that this traditional view is the one held by most preachers who blithely lift up the worshipful abandon of David, while demeaning his wife.

Interestingly, there are feminist scholars who seek to subvert this traditional view by claiming that Michal is set up as a literary foil to David. Ellen White[3] details the history of such interpretation, while Cheryl Exum notes how women in patriarchal texts are frequently made to speak and act against their own interests.[4] In these ways, Michal lacks both agency and subjectivity. The nature of her despising, therefore, is expressed by the patriarchal writer who naturally admonishes David while upbraiding his wife. Could it be that Michal is not a dynamic character filled with intentions that could and should be understood, but that she is merely a literary foil in the hands of the patriarchal writer? Might the reader question David's unabashed, revealing dance if there was not a foil—and a female foil, at that—against which to compare his worshiping actions? Could the purpose of Michal in the text be merely to contrast her lack of worshipfulness with

1. Henry, *Matthew Henry's Commentary*, n.p.
2. Deen, *Wisdom from Women*, 61.
3. White, "Michal the Misinterpreted," 451–64.
4. Exum, "Murder They Wrote."

David's being caught up in the spirit? How might interpretations differ if the roles were reversed? What if Queen Michal, who elsewhere in Scripture is never deemed a "woman after God's own heart," danced and revealed her glory while King David watched from afar and later scolded her worshipful abandon? Perhaps a role reversal would, indeed, reverse the interpretation of traditionalists bound to admonishing the king's every dance step while debasing the despising of his wife.

It is important, therefore, to review the strengths and weaknesses of the traditional theory before moving on to examine the parody theory. As I have made clear, simply demonizing Michal and relegating her to the status of a nagging, unreligious wife who lacks the spirit is a shallow interpretation of the text that confines women into the limited categories of "good or bad" rather than delving into the complexities of their characters. So, the primary weakness of the traditional approach is that it creates an unnecessary binary of Michal as bad and David as good. David's "goodness" could, however, be the traditionalist's primary strength. As indicated by feminists who subvert this theory, it is easy to merely reverse the binary, elevating Michal as the misunderstood victim of the patriarchal writer and debasing David as a raunchy and revealing dancer who disregards Michal's feelings. As we shall see in the theories to come, some of this interpretation of David may be true, but that does not necessarily make his worship any less sincere. By valuing David's worshipful abandon, traditionalists do, indeed, highlight the need for ecstatic worship that throws caution to the wind and simply dances with all might. So, traditionalists teach us that David's wild and worshipful abandon is sincere. At the same time, they unnecessarily devalue the role of the female in the story.

A second theory is the parody theory, which is articulated most fully by Bruce Rosenstock.[5] Much of Rosenstock's analysis finds its foundation in C. L. Seow's work that claims that the return of the ark into Jerusalem draws from elements of mythic narratives celebrating the return of a divine warrior and the installation of said warrior as king.[6] In brief, this theory surmises that David was parodying pan-Mediterranean rituals by "carnivalizing" and subverting the phallic power of YHWH. Michal engaged in ritual abuse language to elicit laughter as a part of carnival. 2 Samuel 6 is an example of sexual subversion because YHWH's glory remains hidden while David's glory is exposed. David, therefore, is deliberately mocking his

5. All references to the parody theory come from Rosenstock, "David's Play," 63–80.
6. See Seow, *Myth, Drama, and the Politics.*

own phallic power. Rosenstock claims that the portrayal of David's dance is utopian because "the narrative of David's dance and self-display can be illuminated against the background of pan-Mediterranean rituals, widely attested in the Greek cultural sphere, involving dance, genital self-display, and mocking speech designed to elicit laughter."[7] In short, the entire narrative exchange and danced event between David and Michal is a parody.

Detailing the exchange between David and Michal is worthwhile in order to understand the premise of the parody theory. The scene proceeds as follows. David, wearing a linen ephod, dances before the Lord with all his might. Michal observes David's dance from a window in the palace and "despises him in her heart." The parody theory hinges on the dialogue that follows. Michal goes out to meet David as he returns to "bless his house" and says, "What glory the king of Israel got for himself today when he was revealed today before the eyes of the servant girls of his subjects just like the way one of those worthless men reveal themselves." Note that Michal begins her statement with the concept of glory. David replies, "Before YHWH— who chose me from my father and his house to appoint me as prince over the people of the Lord, over Israel—I will dance before YHWH. And I will be even more diminished than this. I will be lowly in my own eyes and with the servant girls you spoke, with them I will get myself glory." Note that David ends his statement with the concept of glory. According to Rosenstock's parody theory, David and Michal possess "contrasting views of the nature of divine and royal glory and how they are respectively celebrated and achieved."[8] So, as David seeks to return God's glory by returning the ark of the covenant, so too does he seek to get himself glory by establishing his throne. Rosenstock elaborates further, highlighting the role of "revealing" glory in the parodied ritual:

> Self-exposure is the carnivalization of the subject's pretensions to glory and power. Indeed, we may take David's apparently frontal nudity to be the complete inversion of YHWH's concealment of his glory. Michal is therefore mocking David for seeking to associate the glory of YHWH with his city and his house while debasing his own glory. Of course, Michal also resents the fact that the king's glory, which had only been hers to see, is now shared with

7. Rosenstock, "David's Play," 63.
8. Ibid., 65.

servant girls. But this sexual jealousy should not be understood to
be her sole motivation in making the taunt.[9]

In these ways, the parody theory succeeds in attempting to explain
what can be viewed as a strange way to worship. Dancing in the grips of
God's joy is one thing. Revealing oneself, exposing one's "glory," and full
frontal nudity is another. Being caught up in the unbridled ecstasy of worship can be expected in Scripture. Rationalizing what could be viewed as
a striptease as a form of worship is not quite as expected. In these ways,
the parody theory provides us with some possible answers based on pan-
Mediterranean rituals. At the same time, using the notion of carnival is
anachronistic and an example of reading history backward and using later
rituals to explain an earlier mode of worship. Further, according to Rosenstock, Michal's taunt, though understood as imperative to the ritual parody,
results in her barrenness. Thus, the revealing of David's sexual organs during his dance results in the closing of Michal's.

The sexual nature of the parody theory leads to the third theory behind
David's dancing and Michal's despising. While the third theory addresses a
potential reason behind David's dance, it focuses primarily on why Michal
despised him. That reason is sexual in nature. Delving into David's detailed
sexual dalliances is not the purpose of this chapter, but suffice it to say that
David was a sexually complicated creature.[10]

If we read the entire book of 1 Samuel and the beginning of 2 Samuel
we'll notice that David had a deep and abiding love for someone else before he married Michal. Like the good soap opera that the Bible is, David's
previous lover was none other than Michal's brother, Jonathan. Scripture
is quite clear that David loved Jonathan more than any other woman (2
Sam 1:26). They kissed (1 Sam 20:41) and shared garments and David was
broken when Jonathan died, so broken that he agreed to a political marriage with Jonathan's sister Michal. Susan Ackerman argues that the nar-
rators of 1 and 2 Samuel encrypted same-sex allusions in the texts where
David and Jonathan interact to indicate that the two heroes were lovers.[11] A
lot of heteronormative commentators gloss over this, claiming that David
and Jonathan were the epitome of best friends, but a careful analysis of the
text indicates that they were lovers. And yet David marries Michal and she

9. Ibid., 71.

10. For a thorough analysis of David's sexuality, see Bailey, *David in Love and War*.

11. Ackerman, *When Heroes Love*, 165–231.

despises him. You might also despise someone if you had to marry them when you knew they were actually in love with your dead brother.

Furthermore, even though David was married to Michal, Scripture never mentions that he loves her, only that she loves him (1 Sam 18:20). According to Alter, "This love, twice stated here, is bound to have special salience because it is the only instance in all biblical narrative in which we are explicitly told that a woman loves a man."[12] As such, many scholars propose that David's marriage to Michal was purely political, that David needed Michal in order establish a claim to Saul's throne.[13] On numerous occasions Michal not only states her love for David, she also illustrates her love with actions. In 1 Samuel 19 Michal discovers her father's plot to have David killed and acts out of love to save him. She wakes him, lowers him out of the window, and covers his escape in order to protect him. Even when Michal is later "given" to Paltiel as his wife, there is no mention of her love for him, her agency, or her subjectivity in the narrative. For her heart belongs to David.

All of these sexual intrigues are a part of the lived history that leads David and Michal to their infamous encounter. David has deeply loved her brother. Michal has deeply loved David. David marries Michal for political gain. And the king, who readers know will later abuse his power by taking advantage of a woman (Bathsheba) who inadvertently exposes herself while bathing, has "inadvertently" exposed himself while dancing. The seemingly polyamorous voyeur, the exhibitionist worshiper dances with his sexuality on display for all to see. And the woman who loves him is deeply hurt by these actions. The sincerity of the dance and the intention of the sexual display are not the problem. Rather, Michal feels like a foolish pawn. Ellen White elaborates further: "That she mentions the slave girls at all shows that what is at stake is her role as wife. A woman's status in the home is the only type of status an Israelite woman could gain and Michal held the highest level of status that a woman could get—wife of the king—and yet, her husband has behaved in such a way that has taken what is rightfully hers and given it to any who would look."[14] Accordingly, the sexual theory acknowledges that David's voyeuristic and exhibitionist

12. Alter, *The Art of Biblical Narrative*, 118.

13. Examples include Alter, *The Art of Biblical Narrative*, 120; and Clines, "Michal Observed"; White, "Michal"; Berlin, "Characterization in Biblical Narrative," 24–63, 285–86, and 92–93, respectively, in Clines and Eskenazi, eds., *Telling Queen Michal's Story*.

14. White, "Michal Misinterpreted," 460.

tendencies contribute to his dancing display that "inadvertently" reveals his glory. As we have seen earlier, the wearing of linen ephods is prohibited for these very reasons. Worship with abandon. Get caught up in the spirit. But don't reveal your "glory" while you're dancing before the Lord with all your might. This sexual theory further acknowledges Michal's unending love for a man who uses her as a political pawn, reveals himself to his entire kingdom, and instead loves her brother. According to this theory, is there any wonder why Michal despises David after he dances in this manner?

The fourth and final theory is based solely on the role of dance history in ancient Israelite worship. It is called the communal theory because virtually all dancing in worship for ancient Israelites was communal. Rarely did someone perform a solo dance, but instead all the Israelites would gather together, hand-in-hand to worship YHWH with heart, mind, soul, *and* body. David, therefore, was abusing his power as king by stepping into the worship realm, clad in a forbidden cloth, and dancing about like a soloist. So, rather than demonizing Michal as one who lacked the spirit and would not worship fully like David did, it is important to remember that David was not only revealing "his glory" to anyone who caught a glimpse of his spirit-bound leaps, but he was also leaving others out by making a show of his dance rather than dancing hand-in-hand with his worshiping community. The notion of communal dance is embedded in the Hebrew text, illustrating the primacy of the body in worship.

As detailed in the introduction, we discover ten Hebrew verb forms for the one word "dance" used throughout the Hebrew bible: r*ekad, pazez, mahol, gul, chagag, kirker, dillug, chul, sabab, pasah, siheq*.[15] Ten different words were used to describe our one English word for "dance." This concept seems similar to the way many cultures with cold and snowy climates have multiple words to describe snow; they need a variety of words to describe snow because it is so prevalent in their daily lives. Communal dance was so ingrained in the culture and worship of the ancient Israelites that they needed over ten verb forms to describe it.

Accordingly, when David steps out from the community and puts his dancing worship on display like a soloist, it appears shocking. It's not simply shocking because he reveals his "glory," but because he makes his worship performative rather than communal. In other words, David makes a show of his dancing worship. Dancing in community is a normative practice in ancient Israelite worship; a solo dance is not. If this theory rings

15. Gruber, "Ten Dance-Derived Expressions," 48–66.

true, perhaps Michal is more spiritual and connected to the worshiping community than we might have originally thought. There is little doubt that David was caught in the unbridled ecstasy of worship. The problem is that he was so focused on his own personal worship that he forgot about his worshiping community with his dancing display.

In review, there are four primary theories for why David danced and Michal despised. The traditionalists view David's dance as an authentic form of worship, while Michal's despising was a result of her peevish character. The parody theory views David's dance as satire of pan-Mediterranean ritual, while Michal's despising was part of said ritual's abuse language. The sexual theory views David's dance as that of a sexually fluid exhibitionist flaunting his glory, while Michal's despising is based on her unrequited love for David. And communal theorists view David's dance as a performative solo display that is otherwise unheard of in ancient Israelite worship, while Michal's despising stems from her desire for worship to be communal. Which is correct? That is an excellent question.

I would surmise that the strengths of all of these theories combine to bring readers closer to knowing the intention of David's dance and Michal's despising. I am fairly confident that most interpreters unjustly demonize Michal while ignoring the inadvertent mistakes of David's actions. I am also confident that David was, indeed, caught in a moment of authentic abandon. Ecstatic abandon is often the natural outpouring of worshiping in the grips of God's joy. If David had the foresight, the decorum, or paid enough attention to the feelings of his wife and worshiping community, perhaps he would have prepared his wardrobe differently and avoided the "inadvertent" revelation of his "glory." In these ways, David is worthy of the reprimand many commentators have given his wife over the centuries. Worship *with* your community, David. Be respectful of the feelings of those who care about you, David. But do not curb your enthusiasm. Do not bridle your ecstasy. Dance, David; dance before God with all your might. Next time, however, wear the appropriate clothing.

How David's Dance Can Revolutionize Worship

David's dance can teach us two important things when it comes to worship today. The first is almost silly, and that is to dress appropriately. Now is not the time that I will offer an exposé on the importance of "liturgical" dance clothing with turtlenecks and long sleeves, flowing skirts, and a loose bodice. In fact, I would say the opposite. Judith Rock asserts that the reason "liturgical dance" rarely offers worshipers a glimpse of the holy is because it has insipid theology, choreographic dullness, and a terrible lack of technique.[16] When dancers cloak their bodies in so much fabric that they cannot move and their gestures are hidden, they contribute to a theology that devalues the body, conceals the possibility choreography newness, and hampers any semblance of technique. David's dance, on the other hand, did the opposite: it revealed everything. Rather than reacting so strongly against David's revealing ephod by draping the entire dancing body in so much fabric that the dance is lost, I propose that the dancer strike a balance between the two extremes.

I recall witnessing one of the most moving dances in worship I've ever experienced. An actor performed Baby Suggs's monologue from Toni Morrison's novel, *Beloved*, while a dancer danced and cellist played music. The entire purpose of the monologue is to remind slaves to "love their flesh" and to redeem the black bodies that white masters beat, rape, lynch, and demonize. If the dancer was wearing a standard "liturgical dance" costume with long white sleeves, a full skirt, and loose torso, the message would have been lost. How can you love flesh if all of it is concealed behind fabric? Instead, this dancer's arms, back, and calves were revealed, illustrating strength, grace, beauty, and reminding worshipers of the incarnational and embodied theology their tradition holds so dear. At the same time, if this dancer was wearing nothing but a linen ephod, like King David, I think the message would have also been lost because worshipers would have been distracted by all the "glory" that was being revealed in the sanctuary. In these ways, dancers in worship must choose clothing that allows the body to move freely and that doesn't hide or negate any part of the body. Torsos and hips are just as holy and redeemed as arms and feet, after all. Similarly, dancers should also choose clothing that is not so revealing that leaping and twirling with abandon would result in a wardrobe malfunction like King David.

More important than this, David's dance harkens us back to our primal bodily roots of worship and reminds us of the importance of abandon. David reminds us of the power of the body in worshiping a God who cannot be confined by words, limited by language, or illustrated by image. Texts like this make us recall that our ancestors worshiped God with music, spoken word, and dance, their bodies, hearts, minds, and voices uniting in

16. Rock and Mealey, *Performer as Priest and Prophet.*

a way that was pleasing to God. When we check our bodies at the door and leave worship only to our minds, hearts, and voices, then we are forsaking our history.

The dance of David reminds us that there are times when we become so caught up in the unbridled ecstasy of God's life-changing love that our bodies simply must respond. There are moments when you draw so near to the heart of God that your body cannot contain the joy.

It's important to worship God with your mind. That's why we translate and read historical contexts and exegete. Because the mind is a vital part of our worship. It's important to worship God with your heart. That's why we share personal experiences of why our faith is so meaningful. Because the heart is a vital part of our worship. It's important to worship God with our voices. That's why we sing and pray aloud: because the voice is a vital part of worship. But it's also important to worship God with your body. We are the *body* of Christ, after all. Living, breathing, moving, dancing. Just like David. Because our bodies are holy. Our bodies are redeemed. And when we dance, our bodies worship. There are moments when the most holy thing that can occur is that worshipers draw so near to the heart of God that they dance with utter abandon.

One way that the concept of abandon is best embodied in worship today is through the dances of children. Adults have learned the laws of decorum. Propriety stitches our limbs to our sides for fear of looking foolish. Such is not the case for children. Teaching children simple dances to share in worship is important and valuable, but even more meaningful is allowing children to teach us, the adults. Asking children what worship looks like, how their bodies can shape, image, or act out worship can lead to improvisational holiness. Giving children the open, free, and safe space to move their bodies without fear of being reprimanded can lead to worshiping with abandon.

Once children have paved the way toward worshiping with abandon, adults are often impacted. For example, after children have led worship through dance it could be powerful to invite the congregation to pray. Instead of everyone bowing their heads and contracting their shoulders forward, they could be invited to throw their arms open with wild abandon. Praying takes on a different meaning when the posture of prayer shifts from one of humble decorum to one of wild abandon.

David's dance can revolutionize worship today if only worshipers would realize that their whole bodies—dancing, aching, aging, loving, growing—are capable of abandon. Imagine what worship would look like if we used every part of our body with abandon. Imagine what worship would look like if we cared less about individual propriety and more about communal abandon. Imagine what worship would look like if we were all so caught in the grips of God's joy that our bodies responded by dancing.

CHAPTER 5

The Shulamite's Dance: Passionate Love
Song of Songs 7:1–4

Return, return, the Shulamite.
Return, return, and let us gaze on you.
How will you gaze on Shulamite in the dance of the two camps?
How beautiful are your sandaled feet, O prince's daughter.
The curves of your (quivering?) thighs like jewels crafted by artist hands.
Your vulva¹ a rounded bowl; may it never lack wine.
Your belly a mound of wheat hedged by lotuses.
Your breasts like two fawns . . .

—SONG OF SONGS 7:1–4A²

It is awkward to read these words in relation to the study of religion. Love poetry describing the erotic body, the sensual *female* body, and speaking of—dare we say it—*sexuality* within the confines of faith is beyond taboo. Yet, we hear these words from within the borders of the canon, from the "holy" book that many Jews and Christians claim guides their lives. Despite

1. This Hebrew word is most often translated as "navel," but evidence suggests that in the context of Song of Songs 7:2, the word actually means "vulva." Longman in *Song of Songs*, 194–95 maintains that "navel" is used here as a euphemism. He writes, "The poet says that her '*navel*' never lacks *wine*. The navel is not a particularly moist location, whereas the vulva is, at least when sexually excited . . . This indirect reference to the vulva is in keeping with the poet's strategy of tasteful, though erotic allusions to the woman's body."

2. Translation Mine. Explanation for word choice is elaborated throughout the exegesis.

what some commentators proclaim, the words we hear are not coming from an erotica novel or an X-rated movie;[3] rather, these orgasmic, sensual, bodily words are found within Holy Scripture.

This beautiful dancing woman, this Shulamite, returns to us, her body quivering with delight; and as we read these words, as we gaze upon her voluptuous dancing curves, we must ask ourselves, "What are we to glean from this story hidden deep in the crevices of our sacred canon? Where is God? Is this holy? And if God is *not* found here, if this act of sensuality is *not* holy, then why is this ancient love poem included in the Bible?"

Throughout history, individuals have faithfully exegeted the canticle with a myriad of interpretations. Beginning with Origen,[4] men—predominately celibate priests or monks—have been fascinated with the Song of Songs and interpreted it allegorically, thus taking on the role of the "passive" female and joining Christ and/or God as the bridegroom in holy (and sexual) matrimony. Many go to great lengths, performing hermeneutical gymnastics to interpret the allegory; for example, "the meeting of your thighs" allegorically refers to the coming together of Jews and Gentiles in one church and "your two breasts" as the "two Testaments from which the children begotten in Christ draw milk for their growth."[5]

While many contemporary and feminist scholars critique this allegorical interpretation, queer theorists note the irony of celibate men taking on the female role in the poems, submitting to their "masculine" conceptions of God and, in a divinely satirical manner, managing to "queer" the entire Song with their allegorical understanding. As Stephen Moore notes, "with exquisite irony . . . the austere expositor's attempt to evade the perilous embrace of the woman of the Song plunges him instead into the arms of another love—a male lover, no less, whom he takes to be Christ."[6] Many feminist scholars, while often ascribing to a heteronormative understanding of

3. A primary example of Song of Songs falling into the pornography genre is found in Boer, "Night Sprinkle(s)" 53–70. Here Boer distinguishes Foucault's development of *ars erotica* from *scientia sexualis* along with the development from allegorical to literal interpretation of Song of Songs and dispenses a graphic rendition of the Song *as* a pornographic film through "sexegesis."

4. See Origen, *Homilies on the Song of Songs* in Boer, "Night Sprinkle(s)," 54. Prior to Origen, Hippolytus of Rome is known to have allegorized the Song, but only fragments of the commentary survive.

5. These examples are drawn from Nicholas of Lyra, *The Postilla Litteralis on the Song*, and highlighted in Moore's "The Song of Songs in the History of Sexuality," 333.

6. Moore, "The Song of Songs," 333.

the sexual relations within the Song,[7] also critique the allegorical view and instead highlight the powerful role of the female voice.[8] The women in the Song are not passive bystanders in love or even in sexuality, but instead are the authors, the writers, the dancers, and perhaps even the sexual pursuers. This is not a love poem for the faint of heart. Rather it is a song that pushes the envelope, challenges the status quo, and leaves us wondering if the holy could, indeed, be revealed in our dancing bodies.

And while tomes are written and scholars dedicate their lives to understanding the meaning behind the entire Song of Songs, the task set before us is to interpret the Shulamite's sinuous dance in 7:1–4. So, we repeat these seductive words spoken to the dancer, *shōvoo shōvoo hashulamite*. And these poetic expressions drip off the tongue in pillow-talk fashion as the lover beckons the woman to return and dance again. Marvin Pope contends that this initial word *shōvoo* indicates more than the literal and traditional understanding of the term. Rather than translating *shōvoo* as "return" like most commentators, he interprets the Hebrew to mean "leap."[9] This interpretation stems from the reference to dancing in 7:1d, in addition to Pope's assertion that the repetitive matra, *shōvoo shōvoo*, partnered with emendations involving "revolving, dancing, or leaping" illustrate that the Shulamite is not simply "returning," but leaping in her dance.

As a dancer searching for the origins of sacred dance embedded in the text, this initial discovery fascinated me at first. However, after thoughtful exegesis of the text, I find myself concluding that the Shulamite was likely *not* leaping. My rationale behind this decision, however, does not stem from the Hebrew word etymology or an overall disagreement with Pope's analysis. Rather, like Wendy Buonaventura[10] and other dance historians, I believe that the Shulamite's dance falls into the genre of bellydance and "leaping" is simply not a traditional rhythmic movement in bellydance.[11] Before I continue with an exegesis of Song of Songs 7:1–4, I would like

---

7. For a thorough critique of many feminist's heteronormative understandings of Song of Songs, see Burrus and Moore, "Unsafe Sex," 24–52. Here Burrus and Moore attempt to shift the dualistic and binary interpretations of the Song and instead interpret it through the intersecting lenses of feminist and queer theory.

8. While countless scholars have highlighted the primacy of the female voice in Song of Songs, vital interpreters in this regard begin with Phyllis Trible and continue with much of the work of Athalya Brenner, Cheryl Exum, and Carole Fontaine.

9. Pope, *The Anchor Bible*, 595. Here Pope translates 7:1a as "Leap, leap, O Shulamite."

10. See Buonaventura, *Belly Dancing*, 20.

11. I discuss the movements of traditional bellydance and how these movements are found in Song of Songs 7:1–4 in detail later.

to explore some of the sacred origins of bellydance and how these origins relate to the Song.

Origins of Bellydance: A Sacred History

In order to faithfully place the Shulamite's dance in the genre of bellydance, it is first imperative to explore some of the origins of the sacred in bellydance. I will return to a proper exegesis of 7:1–4 after expounding upon the history of the sacred in bellydance. First, I will explore a brief history of bellydance, although there is much scholarly dispute regarding the beginnings of this dance form. Second, I will investigate three sacred concepts present throughout the history of bellydance and potentially manifest in Song of Songs 7:1–4. These three categories are interrelated, yet I divide them into the following sections: 1) bellydance and sexuality, 2) bellydance and childbirth, and 3) bellydance and goddess worship.

History of Bellydance: Ancient Origins, Ghawazi, and Ouled Nail

In the beginning, Eurynome, the Goddess of All Things, rose naked from Chaos, but found nothing substantial for her feet to rest upon, and therefore divided the seas from the sky, dancing lonely upon its waves. She danced towards the south, and the wind set in motion behind her seemed nothing new and apart with which to begin a work of creation. Wheeling about, she caught hold of the north wind, rubbed it between her hands, and behold! the great serpent Ophion. Eurynome danced to warm herself, wildly and more wildly, until Ophion, grown lustful, coiled about those divine limbs and was moved to couple with her. So Eurynome was got with child. Next, she assumed the form of a dove, brooding the waves, and in due process of time, laid the Universal Egg. At her bidding, Ophion coiled several times about this egg until it hatched and split in two. Out tumbled all things that exist, her children: sun, moon, planets, stars, the earth with its mountains and rivers, its trees, herbs, and living creatures.[12]

Many dance historians and scholars of bellydance believe that its mythic origins are embedded in the creation narrative. As such, the Goddess Eurynome dances as a paradigm for all bellydancers from the dawn of time, giving birth to the universe through her sensual dance. Daniela Gioseffi

12. Graves, *The Pelasgian Creation Myth*, 27.

furthers this creation concept by noting that some of the earliest historical evidence that supports bellydance are Upper Paleolithic cave paintings illustrating the goddess Venus.[13] According to Gioseffi, these paintings point toward matriarchal societies where the female body is worshiped for its child-bearing capacities. She develops this ancient history further by pointing toward the Neolithic Era where dancers with shaking hips are painted in tomb paintings.

Bellydancing was kept alive because it was not limited to one country or culture. Rather, bellydance continued through the traveling of gypsies, possibly coming from India and migrating west to Europe. Some gypsiologists believe the word "Rom" or "Romany" (used to described gypsies) derives from the Sanskrit "Dom," which is an Indian caste that earned its livelihood from singing and dancing.[14] After leaving India in the fifth century CE the gypsies made their way across land routes through Afghanistan, which linked them to the Middle East. They likely divided on the shores of the Mediterranean, some going to present-day Turkey, Iran, and Greece and others going to Egypt and the northern shores of Africa. They went as far as Spain where bellydance developed into the flamenco, and some would speculate the Romany gypsies traveled as far as France. The gypsies performed remnants of the old birth mime and, in order to make a living, transformed ritual dance into entertainment.[15]

The two most documented groups of dancing gypsies were the Ghawazi and the Ouled Nail. In Egyptian villages a professional dancer is known as a Ghawazi.[16] The origins of the Ghawazi are unknown, but according to Stewart, an image on the wall of an early Eighteenth Dynasty tomb of Neb Amon attests to their potential antiquity.[17] The Ghawazi are not actually of Egyptian descent, but some believe that they may be part of the Indo-Persian traveling gypsies that migrated from northern India. In Egyptian, Ghawazi actually means "invaders" or "outsiders" as gypsies have

13. Gioseffi does not provide more than a listed chronology (*Earth Dancing*, 42–48) of bellydancing without much explanation. Her presumptions are grounded in the relation to goddess worship embedded in bellydance's history, which nearly all dance historians agree upon, and on which I will elucidate further in the "Bellydance and Goddess Worship" section.

14. Buonaventura, *Belly Dancing*, 5.

15. I will further develop the concept of the birth mime in my section on "Bellydancing and Child Birth."

16. Buonaventura, *Serpent of the Nile*, 39.

17. Stewart, *Sacred Woman*, 88.

always lived on the fringes of society.[18] Tina Hobin further notes that the name Ghawazi can literally translate as "invader of the heart" or "thieves of the heart."[19] Not only were the Ghawazi "outsiders" traveling into the margins of new societies, but they were also known as seductresses capable of capturing the hearts of men.

While the Ghawazi roamed and lived on the outskirts of society, sometimes individuals were hired to dance for festivities. The payment and reputation of dancers depended on the status of their patrons. For example, Ghawazi bellydancers performing in Egypt during the Fourth Dynasty (2680–2560 BCE) were rewarded with precious jewels and gold necklaces while performers in the marketplace settled for coins tossed at their feet. Having nowhere to stow their earnings, dancers incorporated them into their wardrobe, hemming them onto skirts and sashes or sewing the coins into their head coverings or shawls.[20] As such, many professional dancers were the breadwinners for their families, a freedom not traditionally permitted to other women. In fact, many Moroccan bellydancers developed the reputation of "women who do not want men to tell them what to do."[21] According the Buonaventura, bellydancers were considered fortunate in some respects as "they were not obliged to conform to all the rules of society. Their work gives them social mobility and independence, and though their position may be ambivalent, that in itself can be a kind of freedom."[22] These dancers were rather capable of supporting themselves or their families and were empowered by their ancient goddess belief systems. The heart of Ghawazi belief is in the Hindu tradition and their patron saint is the Indian goddess Kali, the Black Madonna.[23] Thus, Ghawazi bellydancers may have lived on the margins of society, shunned as women who use their bodies to earn money, but they were also competent women in charge of their own sexuality and livelihood, which was not typical of any other female profession during this time.

The Ouled Nail of Algeria is another group of mysterious origins. In contrast to the negative attitudes and stigma directed at the Ghawazi, the Ouled Nail dancers were rarely disrespected. As inhabitants of Marabout

18. Buonaventura, *Serpent of the Nile*, 39.

19. Hobin, *Belly Dance*, 104.

20. Buonaventura, *Serpent of the Nile*, 44.

21. Ibid., 51.

22. Ibid., 52.

23. Ibid., 39.

and descendants of a saint, the Algerian Mohammedans accepted the profession as the Ouled Nail as a religious rite.[24] These unveiled public bellydancers of the Sahara Djurdjura were famous for their jeweled crowns, or *zeriref*, and their reputations proceeded them as far back as the sixth century BCE.[25] These *zeriref* crowns were made of silver and gold coins and decorated with turquoise, coral, and colored enamels. Consequently, Ouled Nail dancers were famous for wearing their payments as jewelry and decoration, much like Ghawazi dancers. Often they wore arm bangles studded with pins and points, which protected them against thieves and attackers.[26] Under layers of jewels, belts, and caftans, their dance features the *danse du ventre*, a rhythmic "rolling" of the abdominal muscles.[27]

Ouled Nail dancers began their training at a very young age and once they were married they rarely returned to their profession. After traveling, women earn their dowries by dancing, which has little effect on their reputations at home in this particular culture. Then they return to their village to marry and live according to Muslim society. Once women were married they only continued to dance within the confines of other women rather than as performance.

Both the Ghawazi and Ouled Nail bellydancers paved the way for what is referred to today as *raqs baladi*, literally "native dance." *Raqs baladi* was and is particularly strong in Egypt. The "native dance" is an earthy, feminine dance of the hips and pelvis. There is rarely a social event, such as a wedding, circumcision ritual, or religious festival where this form of bellydance is not present.[28] *Raqs sharqi*, on the other hand, is a professional version of *raqs baladi* that is performed in contemporary nightclubs and cabarets. In keeping with the notions of bellydancing at weddings, circumcision rituals, and religious festivals, I will now explore the role of bellydance in three similar venues: 1) bellydance and sexuality, 2) bellydance and childbirth, and 3) bellydance and goddess worship.

24. Hobin, *Belly Dance*, 126.

25. Stewart, *Sacred Woman*, 89.

26. Al-Rawi, *Grandmother's Secrets*, 45.

27. Stewart, *Sacred Woman*, 89.

28. Al-Rawi, *Grandmother's Secrets*, 45.

Bellydance and Sexuality

"We have been making its movements as long as we have been making love, so we could say the dance is as old as life itself."[29]

Based simply on the serpentine movements, the rolling of the abdomen, and the shimmying of the hips, it is evident that bellydance and sexuality are inextricably linked. The dance imitates sexual movements and is, therefore, a sexual dance. However, the role of sexuality in bellydance is much deeper than mere imitation. Rather, the bellydance is related to female wedding rituals, a mother's search for a perfect daughter-in-law, female exploration within harems, and even spiritual sexual empowerment. Therefore, I will explore each of these facets of bellydance and sexuality separately.

First, I will expound upon the role of bellydance in wedding rituals. Dance historian Daniela Gioseffi reminds us of the role of *awalem*, or "those who teach."[30] Traditionally, the *awalem* were dancers, reminiscent of earlier fertility dancers, who were hired to attend weddings for the purpose of "hinting, stimulating, or initiating the bride and groom into what should occur in the wedding bed that night."[31] The sinuous movements of the bellydancer were intended to teach women how to move sexually. Similarly, Iris Stewart describes the *scheikha* in Moroccan weddings, also known as *hannana* in Egyptian weddings.[32] These dancers oversee the seven days of women's ceremonies and rituals before the wedding and bestow her blessing on the bride. In addition to entertaining the female guests, the *scheikha* dances in front of the bride, singing verses about the pleasures of marital relations that await after the ordeal of the wedding night and loss of her virginity. Thus, she dances with exaggerated hip and stomach movements, teaching the bride how to move her own body.

Furthermore, the bride was thought to be especially vulnerable to evil spirits during her transition from girlhood to womanhood. So, trancelike bellydances were used to banish these malevolent spirits and to release

29. Buonaventura, *Belly Dancing,*, 2.

30. Gioseffi, *Earth Dancing*, 39.

31. Ibid.

32. All subsequent descriptions of bellydance in wedding preparation come from Stewart, *Sacred Woman*, 90–91 unless otherwise noted.

negative energies, providing an atmosphere of calm and well-being.[33] Hajja Noura Durkee refers to this type of dancing as "sexual meditation."[34]

Not only is bellydance used to teach brides about sexuality, but it is also a way in which mothers search for brides-to-be. In this vein, Rosina-Fawzia Al-Rawi recounts her childhood memories of learning bellydance as she tells the stories of the many times women and girls gathered together for parties or prayer apart from men. Bellydancing was always present at such gatherings. Everyone would dance and take turns coming to the center of the room to "perform" for the other women. Mothers-in-law used this opportunity to decide on future daughters-in-law based on their body movements; single women knew that their bellydancing in female gatherings had the potential to determine their futures. Al-Rawi notes that in such gatherings little girls danced, single and married women danced, but the most memorable was when the older women danced. "Suddenly," Al-Rawi states, "something was there that could not be expressed in words—a gift, a woman's prayer filled the room, born by the subtle, nearly wise movements of one who stood far ahead of us in the long chain of women. So when an old woman got up to dance and show her mature sensuality and her old beauty, we kissed her hands gratefully."[35] Thus, the older women took on a similar role as the *awalem* in such gatherings as they searched for potential brides for their sons while also teaching the "girls" how to dance like real women, with maturity and fullness.

Clearly, it is evident that the role of sexuality in bellydance was prevalent in weddings and in the search for suitable brides. But bellydancing was also sexually charged within female harems. Within the confines of the harem, dancing was one of the few avenues of sexual expression allowed for women.[36] Interestingly, the Turkish word for harem comes from the Arabic *haram/haruma*, which means "off limits," "disallowed," "illegal," and even "holy" or "unbreakable."[37] Only women and eunuchs were permitted within a harem. And while some harems were "off limits" places where sultans reserved women for his pleasure, the majority of the time, harems were "off limits" places where women spent their days with other women and away

---

33. Buonaventura, *Serpent of the Nile*, 160.

34. Stewart, *Sacred Woman*, 91.

35. Al-Rawi, *Grandmother's Secrets*, 21.

36. All descriptions of bellydance in harems come from Buonaventura, *Belly Dancing*, 58 unless otherwise noted.

37. Coluccia et al., *Belly Dancing*, 44.

from any men. As such, women filled their days talking with other women, dancing, singing, possibly learning musical instruments, and exploring their sexuality with other women. Often women used bellydancing as a way of staging imitations of the sexual act, sometimes engaging in lesbian sex, as one dancer assumed the role of the "man" in the sexual imitation dance. Within the harem the dance became an art performed by women largely for their own sex in forced seclusion. While women were forced into harems, they often became a haven for sexual intrigue among females, a safe place to explore one's sexuality through dance with other women. Much contemporary bellydance in the Middle East still takes place in seclusion from men, with women dancing with and for one another.

Thus, it is clear that bellydance was used as an avenue for exploring one's sexuality with other women, searching for a suitable daughter-in-law, and as training for brides. Additionally, the sexual elements of bellydance took on a sacred appeal. And according to Buonaventura, these sexual dances were related to worship. "It was once found throughout the world, a dance in which movement of the hips—sometimes vigorous, sometimes soft and sinuous—was the principal expression. Originally it had a precise meaning in terms of ritual and ceremony, for it expressed the mysteries of life and death as people understood them then."[38] And while the attitude of the Arab world toward dance was ambivalent, Islam disapproved of mixed dancing; a dance that radiates such strong erotic energy and furthers the feminine sexual force should simply not be performed in public, according to the Muslim tradition. "While acknowledging the power of the feminine, Islam sees it as a potentially disruptive factor, unless it be controlled by rules and regulations—hence the use of the veil, the segregation of the sexes, and practice of isolation." [39] In the midst of these regulations, however, women were permitted to bellydance among other women; they did it for their own pleasure and used it in their daily lives and in their ceremonies. "As long as the dance had been part of a religious ritual, no male audience had ever been allowed."[40]

Bellydance has historically been a mode through which brides learned how to move sexually during the wedding ceremony. It has also served as a litmus tests for mothers searching for brides for their sons; the more sinuous the dancer was, the better wife and mother she would be. Furthermore,

---

38. Buonaventura, *Serpent of the Nile*, 10–11.

39. Al-Rawi, *Grandmother's Secrets*, 43.

40. Ibid.

bellydance posed as a method of sexual exploration for women confined to harems. And this sexually charged dance proved sacred, a way for women to move their bodies in accord with the earth. In this section I have explored the relationship between bellydance and sexuality and I will now illuminate the connection between bellydance and childbirth.

Bellydance and Childbirth

In ancient Egypt, the ab, one of the seven souls, was supposed to come directly from the mother's heart, in the form of holy lunar blood that descended into her womb to take the shape of her child. The hieroglyphic sign for this eminently matriarchal idea was a dancing figure, representing the inner dance of life perceived in the heartbeat. As long as the dance continued, life went on.[41]

According to Tina Hobin, "it is believed that bellydance may be one of the oldest dance forms and that it developed from the fertility dances of the mother goddess cult."[42] Janice Crosby further notes that origins of bellydance are associated with pre-patriarchal times, relating to birthing rituals and fertility rites as a celebration of feminine principles.[43] In prehistoric societies it was unusual for women to participate in animal magic or hunting dances like men; however, women were always the leaders in fertility rituals and birth dances, including the bellydance.[44] Sexuality clearly played a significant role in bellydance, but so, too, did childbirth. The ancient birth mime is a type of dance in which women mimetically act out the birthing process—rolling abdomens, rotating the hips and pelvis, and squatting into the knees—and bellydance is a derivative of this ancient mime. Furthermore, the movements of bellydance strengthen the abdomen and pelvis muscles, thus making the process of childbirth less painful. The dance is also used as a hypnotic or focusing tool during labor, an ancient prototype of lamas of sorts.

Many women in Middle Eastern cultures surround a woman in labor, bellydancing, in order to hypnotize her into relaxing into her contractions. The floor-work portion of bellydance mirrors many birthing maneuvers, and it is easy to theorize that the floor work in bellydance is actually a remnant

41. Walker, *The Woman's Dictionary*, 72.

42. Hobin, *Belly Dance*, 21.

43. Crosby, "The Goddess Dances," 168.

44. Hobin, *Belly Dance*, 21.

of the ancient birth mime.[45] Saudi Arabian dancer Farab Firdoz confirms that bellydance has roots in the birth mime. She learned the dance from her grandmother who told her that its slower movements, which concentrate on the abdominal muscles, derive from one of the oldest religious dances that imitate a woman's birth contractions: "She told me that as recently as twenty-five years ago, she had been present when the women of her grandmother's tribe gathered around the pallet of a woman in labour [sic] and did these movements, encouraging her to do them too, rendering the birth less painful. Other dances were done afterwards, to celebrate the birth, as well as a more elaborate repetition of the actual birth mime."[46] In a similar vein, Iris Stewart recounts the story of a group of women in a Moroccan birth ritual where the dancers surrounded a pregnant woman, undulating their abdomens while moving slowly in a clockwise circle around her. The mother would squat into contractions and then stand up and join the women in the bellydance, returning again to contractions until she gave birth to twins.[47]

Armenian dancer, Armen Ohanian elaborates more regarding the connections between bellydance and childbirth:

> It was [a dance] of the mystery and pain of motherhood . . . In olden Asia which has kept the dance in its primitive purity, it represents the mysterious conception of life, the suffering and joy with which a new soul is brought into the world. Could any man born of woman contemplate this most holy subject expressed in an art so pure and so ritualistic as our eastern dance, with less than profound reverence? Such is our Asiatic veneration of motherhood, that there are countries and tribes whose most binding oath is sworn upon the stomach, because it is from this sacred cup that humanity has issued.[48]

Traditionally, during this ritualistic dance, men are not allowed to be present. It is rather a dance for women by women. Bellydancing in such contexts provided a safe space for women to explore their sexuality, discover the beauty and connectedness of childbirth, and become empowered as women in community. Janice Crosby expounds upon the connection between bellydance as a part of birthing rituals and female-empowerment

45. Gioseffi, *Earth Dancing*, 28.

46. Varga-Dinicu, "A Criticism of Nadia Gamal," 22.

47. Stewart, *Sacred Woman*, 81–82.

48. Ohanian, *La Danseuse de Shamakha*, 72.

as she associates feminism with nonviolent philosophies that nurture the earth when she states, "Not only does the earth give birth to us, but we give birth to ourselves, to our own identities through the acts and behavior patterns of our lives as we live them, moment to moment, alive in the present, seeing, feeling, touching, tasting, hearing, and smelling what is good and worthy and right in terms of our actions and pleasures."[49]

Thus, it is clear that bellydance and childbirth have vital connections manifest in the remnants of the ancient birth mime, the role of the dance as a hypnotic focusing-point during birth, and even as a way to strengthen the muscles in order to prevent pain in labor. Furthermore, the way in which bellydance and childbirth are connected is also a way of building community among women and empowering their connection to each other and the earth. I have illustrated the associations between bellydance and sexuality and childbirth. Now, I would like to elucidate the way in which bellydance and goddess worship are inextricably linked.

Bellydance and Goddess Worship

Tying together the notions of sacred sexuality and childbirth, Janice Crosby proposes that this bellydance can be seen in the context of "Goddess spirituality that not only celebrates the female body, but also serves as a medium of embodying the archetypal feminine power."[50] She elaborates that a significant portion of bellydancers and other Middle Eastern dancers go beyond espousing the art as a sensuous expression of female grace and power; "they see it as charged with spiritual signification, most often in the form of association with Goddess imagery."[51] As bellydancing was almost always performed in the context of women—namely mothers, daughters, daughters-in-law, grandmothers—this endless succession of women became "mortal representatives of the Great Mother Earth, and the movements of their dancing reflected this."[52] Furthermore, what I have earlier referenced as the "birth mime" was part of goddess rites in the prehistoric world.[53] Actually, a major characteristic of all prehistoric matriarchal cults was dancing as it was the most important magical practice of all. Danc-

---

49. Crosby, "The Goddess Dances," 168.

50. Ibid., 170.

51. Ibid., 166.

52. Al-Rawi, *Grandmother's Secrets*, 30.

53. Buonaventura, *Belly Dancing*, 23.

ing is the oldest and most elementary form of spiritual expression and all other art forms have developed from dancing.[54] In the pages that follow I explore the connection between bellydance and goddess worship as seen in ancient goddess mythology, priestess dances, moon dances, and as a way for women to embody the goddess.

First I will examine the connection between bellydance and goddess mythology. From the earliest cultures of the Paleolithic Era to the Neolithic Era there is evidence that diverse forms of dance, such as the bellydance, and fertility dances were linked to earth mother goddess worship.[55] The bellydance is believed to the be the oldest form of dance, evolving from worship of the great mother goddess and growing out of a combination of fertility cults, religious rituals, and magic dances of ancient civilizations.[56] Some origin stories place bellydancing in the context of ancient Sumerian and Egyptian goddess worship and connect the dance to the goddesses Isis and Ishtar. Sandstone reliefs over three thousand years old in Sakkara picture dancers moving their hips. These reliefs likely depict festival dancing to honor Isis in ancient Egypt.[57] Additionally, the Greek goddess of carnal love, Aphrodite, performed a solo dance called the *cifte telli*; contemporary Greek bellydance is still known by this name. Furthermore, the *cifte telli* was popular throughout the eastern Mediterranean where worship of the moon goddess was the strongest. It is described as a dance full of swaying, undulating movements with shaking shoulders, quivering hips, and arm movements like those of snakes.[58]

One of the oldest archetypes of the Great Mother was Ishtar. This Babylonian goddess symbolized, on the one hand, the earth and fertility, and, on the other hand, death and destruction. According to Al-Rawi, "she was often represented with burning eyes, the symbol of light and spirit, and a burning navel, the symbol of fertility and death. In these representations, the earth, which is taken as feminine reality, is the body, and its center is the navel, from which the world receives nourishment."[59] By dancing with the naval as the central focus, bellydancers are embodying Ishtar's ability

---

54. Al-Rawi, *Grandmother's Secrets*, 29.

55. Hobin, *Belly Dance*, 20.

56. Ibid., 95.

57. Coluccia et al., *Belly Dancing*, 14.

58. Buonaventura, *Belly Dancing*, 22.

59. Al-Rawi, *Grandmother's Secrets*, 30.

to nourish the world. Ishtar is regarded as the goddess who initiated the Dance of the Seven Veils:

> When Ishtar's husband, Tammouz, died and returned to the world of darkness, the womb of the earth, Ishtar decided to save him by craft and to bring back the light. She dressed up in all her splendor, tied a girdle around her hips and donned seven veils to enter the netherworld through seven gates. The goddess of love danced seductively at each gate, each time leaving one veil to gain entrance. At the seventh gate, she removed the last veil. During the whole of her stay in the underworld, all life on earth stood still, deprived of love, growth, and celebration. Only when Ishtar returned, fully veiled to shield her secret from human eyes, did life on earth blossom again. Her reunion with Tammouz was celebrated every year at the beginning of spring and symbolized the reawakening of nature and life.[60]

It is proposed that Ishtar's seduction dance was one of the beginnings of bellydance and, reciprocally, when women tie a girdle or scarf around their hips it reminds us of Ishtar's dance and transforms today's woman into an interpreter of a culture long ago.[61]

Not only are goddesses remembered as bellydancers or recipients of dancing worship, but temple priestesses are known for bellydancing in some contexts. For example, Indian temple priestesses performed erotic dances that included pelvic undulations;[62] these dancers also sometimes engaged in sacred temple prostitution. However, when a temple priestess had sexual relations she was engaging in a sacred rite, not selling a sexual commodity in the marketplace. According to Wendy Buonaventura, when the priestess danced, she performed with her back to the worshipers, making sinuous movements, not for the people, but for the deity, represented in the effigy before her.[63] This dancing released energy in her body and this energy enabled her to unite with the divine spirit. Thus, she was seen as a sacred force and sexual encounters with such dancers were like having a sexual encounter with the divine. Furthermore, at the great temple of the goddess Artemis in Ephesus, priestesses worshiped in ecstatic mystery rites that included dancing. According to the Greek traveler Pausanius, their

60. This story of Ishtar's Dance of the Seven Veils is found in Neumann, *The Great Mother*, 167.

61. Al-Rawi, *Grandmother's Secrets*, 32.

62. Buonaventura, *Belly Dancing*, 25.

63. Ibid., 26.

dance was one of great antiquity whose essential characteristic was a rotation of the hips and abdomen; this dance was known as the *kordax*.[64]

The role of bellydance in goddess mythology and priestess dances is also similar to the role of bellydance as a moon dance. Since the influence of the moon on the feminine cycle was so well-known, it is not surprising that women gathered for rituals once a month. These blood and fertility rituals happened during the night, to the exclusion of men. The places chosen for such rituals were usually hills or other elevated places. The hills symbolize the feminine, as they rise gently above the earth, like the belly. And it was on top of the hill—on the navel of the earth—that women of the primitive societies danced. These dances revolved around fertility and therefore the belly played a major part. "The dances were used to strengthen sexual energy, to awaken joy, and to praise the mysteries of life. The women danced their dance, a dance that corresponded to their body and expressed all the moods and feelings, all the longings, sufferings, and joys of being a woman. Through their dance, they came into harmony with the universe, abandoning themselves to life and to the divine."[65] And women did this in the presence of one another and the moon.

Thus, bellydance is similar to ancient moon dances and it also serves as way for women to embody their inner goddess. According to Janice Crosby, "Envisioning the dances as an ancient female tradition which celebrates the Mother Goddess and women as celebrants/teachers allows many dancers to see themselves as embodying the divine female, while at the same time this position puts women in a superior stance to those who would like to see the dance as something which 'naughty' women do to titillate men."[66] Furthermore, the general focus on the dance is one suited to the female body because of its circular and flowing movements. "If one looks at the Goddess in an archetypal rather than historical sense, bellydance's emphasis on the art form as embodying female attributes such as creation and sensuality also links it to Goddess spirituality's idea of all women as goddesses."[67] Therefore, bellydance becomes a way for women to embody their own inner goddess.

Along the lines of embodying or becoming-one-with the goddess, bellydancer Baraka, writes, "for me, dance is prayer—prayer for greater

---

64. Ibid., 22.
65. Al-Rawi, *Grandmother's Secrets*, 33.
66. Crosby, "The Goddess Dances," 168.
67. Ibid., 169.

understanding, for compassion, for gentleness and humility, for growth, for fellowship, for a better world. When I dance, I touch the face of the Goddess."[68] Moreover, Sharon Andres, an ordained Methodist minister and practitioner of bellydance echoes Baraka's sentiments when she states, "there is an almost sacramental aspect to this self-celebration. Joyous, ecstatic, passionate, and sensual, the dance says that bodies created in the image of the Divine are worth loving, physically, spiritually, and erotically."[69]

Hence, it is clear that bellydance and goddess worship are closely linked. This connection is evident in ancient goddess mythology, priestess dances, moon dances, and as a way for women to embody the goddess. In these examples, bellydance served as a life-affirming, body-empowering medium for women to connect with the goddess within and the ancient historical and archetypal goddess. But what has happened to these links in contemporary bellydance? While many modern bellydancers still ascribe to goddess ideologies and use bellydance in a similar manner as women throughout ancient history, it is worthwhile to touch upon some of the brief shifts that have changed bellydance from a woman-empowering dance to a dance often equated with stripping. While these shifts are not particularly applicable to the Shulamite's dance, they are still worthy of our consideration since we are contemporary readers reflecting on the text in our own patriarchal context.

As religion and society shifted from matriarchy to patriarchy, lunar to solar, cyclical to linear, the forms of worship and ritual also shifted. The adherents to goddess religions were forced to withdraw from the public sphere, although likely still practicing their beliefs and dances. As time passed, the meanings behind these ancient goddess rituals were obscured. Although most priestesses were banished as witches or harlots, the birth magic rituals persisted as a ceremonial necessity in marriages, and birth and circumcisions.[70] In many contemporary cases, the ancient woman-affirming ritual dance has been subverted to male voyeurism. Al-Rawi elaborates on this transition:

> The transition from matriarchal to patriarchal society was taking place and this was reflected in the dancing culture. During official events, dance came to be performed mainly by the ruling class, kings, and priests, while women were only allowed to dance for

68. Ibid., 178.

69. Ibid.

70. Stewart, *Sacred Woman*, 93.

the entertainment of the higher social classes. Women's loss of social power manifested itself in their restricted freedom of movement as well as in the new functions of their dances. For the first time, we find evidence of professional dancers, girls and women, performing for the entertainment of others, which further demonstrates the transition from the sacred to the profane, to dancing as a show. Ritual dances involving the whole community were replaced by entertainment dances performed by professionals . . . Although women's dance retained many original elements, it lost its sacred meaning when it aimed solely to satisfy male curiosity, a change which has survived to a large extent to this very day.[71]

Amidst this transition, dancers are encouraged by reconnecting bellydance to its goddess ancestry, so that we can look to a future where all women may dance divinely. The areas of "goddess history" combined with the issues of body image, sexuality, and spirituality reveal connections with the goddess movement which have allowed women to return to the origins of this dance tradition in a way generally prohibited for women in its countries of origin.[72] Thus, bellydance has subversive potential in an otherwise patriarchal society.

It is worthy to note that the role of bellydance in all three categories—sexual training, childbirth, and goddess worship—were places where women dance with or for other women. The majority of the time the dance was performed amidst a female community where little girls were raised learning the dance from other women and girls. Men were rarely present unless a professional bellydancer was hired for entertainment; and this style of bellydance does not fit neatly into one of the three expounded upon categories. Within the confines of harems or female rituals, the distinction between performer and spectator was blurred. Rather, women danced while others watched and then the roles reversed. All were provided the opportunity to dance.

Thus, it is evident that the ancient art of bellydance, as likely seen in Song of Songs 7, is not the same as nightclub performances of bellydance in contemporary culture where women are the object of the male gaze. Rather, this type of bellydance was performed by women in the context of women and in relation to sacred sexuality, childbirth, and goddess worship. And with these sacred origins of bellydance now established I shall return to the Shulamite's dance.

71. Al-Rawi, *Grandmother's Secrets*, 36–37.
72. Crosby, "The Goddess Dances," 167.

Returning to the Shulamite, Yet Again[73]

Now that I have developed a foundational understanding of bellydancing's sacred origins, I return to the Shulamite's dance from Song of Songs 7:1–4. First, let us return to examine the concept of "the dance of two camps" from 7:1d. The origin of the word for dance in 7:1d is *mahol*. According to Julian Morganstern, the "fundamental meaning of the stem *hol* is 'to revolve in a circle,' 'to turn,' while in Hebrew 'to dance' is the simplest meaning of the word."[74] He believes that the likelihood of the original meaning of this stem was "to be round," and from the secondary meaning, "to revolve in a circle," "to turn," and "to dance," evolved.[75]

As the women throughout the Song describe themselves as keepers of the vineyard, every vineyard in ancient Israel had a *mahol*, "etymologically a dancing-place."[76] Bertinoro notes that, in this *mahol* maidens of Israel used to celebrate their vineyard dances, implying the regular commemoration of the annual festival when the women of Shiloh came forth to dance in the vineyards. The Mishna provides more detailed information that is worthy of recounting at length:

> The maidens of Jerusalem used to go out, clad in white garments, that had been borrowed, in order not to put to shame those who had none. All these garments had to be previously dipped in water. And the maidens of Jerusalem would go out and dance in the vineyards. And what would they say? "Young man, lift thine eyes and see whom thou wilt choose. Set not thine eyes upon beauty, but upon family . . ." The Mishna states very closely that these dances were celebrated twice a year . . . [This] indicates that in the ancient Israelite and pre-Israelite form of the ceremony the young men regularly stood by, openly or concealed in the vineyards, as were the Benjaminites, and at the proper moment stepped forth and seized, each the maiden of his choice, to become his partner in sacred sexual intercourse for the night, and his wife and the mother of his children for the future.[77]

73. "Returning to the Shulamite, Yet Again" is a direct quote from Athalya Brenner's article title, but is a fitting section title after a substantial time away from the text. I have thus explored the history of bellydance and now I return to Song of Songs 7:1–4.

74. Morgenstern, "Etymological History," 321.

75. Ibid., 321.

76. Ibid., 324.

77. Cited in ibid., 324–35.

From a feminist perspective this word usage illustrating a wet T-shirt dance of sorts could likely make some uncomfortable. There is, at the same time, however, also goddess worship associated with this term. Together with sacred sexual intercourse, these *mahol* dances, were "in origin undoubtedly homeopathic magical rites, celebrated in the worship of the ancient Semitic mother-goddess, and were designed to promote fertility of vineyards and fields."[78] Additionally, according to Gruber, *mahol* is also interpreted as a whirling dance in which the dancer rotates and "thereby exhibits her beauty" to prospective marriage partners.[79]

In this regard, Wetzstein proposes that the Shulamite's dance is similar to that of contemporary wedding dances in Syria. Wetzstein describes a bellydance in which the bride wielded a sword on the wedding day surrounded by a ring of people, one half composed of men and the other half composed of women, thus explaining the "two camps" reference.[80] Or perhaps, according to Albright, the "dance of the two camps/armies" is a prototype referring to the war goddess Shulmanitu, or Ishtar, the patroness of warriors, or the goddess Anath,[81] also likening the Shulamite's dance to ancient bellydance.

After the lover beckons the dancing Shulamite to "return" as the subject[82] of our gaze, a poetic flow of words follows. These words fall into the genre known as a wasf, or Arabic love poem.[83] Traditionally, wasfs describe female beauty, and the Song contains three of such poems (4:1–5; 5:10–16; 7:1–7). However, the poetry from chapter 7 is different from its predecessors due to the reverse order of descriptive beauty, namely that the lover describes the Shulamite from toe to head rather than the traditional reverse (head to toe).[84] This descriptive reversal is perhaps dictated by the situation: when a woman dances, her feet are called to attention first.

78. Ibid., 327.

79. Gruber, "Ten Dance-Derived Expressions," 57.

80. Wetzstein as cited in Pope, *The Anchor Bible*, 604.

81. See Albright, "Archaic Survivals in the Text of Canticles."

82. I intentionally refer to the Shulamite here as the "subject" of the gaze rather than the "object" of the gaze. While some commentators, possibly Fiona Black, contend that the woman is objectified and satirized in 7:1–8, I interpret the text as one of mutual love where the Shulamite is described as beautiful out of love and admiration rather than objectification.

83. Brenner, "'Come Back, Come Back The Shulammite.'" 251.

84. Brenner, *The Song of Songs*, 44.

It is worthy to note the bodily progression of described beauty. The lover begins by doting on the Shulamite's beautiful sandaled feet, and moves upward to her curved thighs, rounded vulva, quivering belly, breasts, neck, and face. Within this wasf category, we discover strikingly similar bodily description poems, such as the tale in *One Thousand and One Nights*:

> The . . . damsel . . . was the loveliest creature Allah had made in her day, and indeed she outdid in beauty all human beings . . . her middle was full of folds, a dimpled plain . . . and her navel an ounce of musk, sweetest of savour could contain. She had thighs great and plump, like marble columns twain or bolsters stuffed with down . . . and between them a somewhat, as it were a hummock great of span of a hare with ears back lain . . . and indeed she surpassed . . . with her beauty and symmetry.[85]

In both wasfs we read the description of a beautiful woman, a woman with "curved" or "plump" thighs, a rounded "vulva/navel," a belly like a "mound of wheat" or "dimpled plain," "full of folds." And in our contemporary American culture that idealizes the emaciated and youthful body of models, we may read these descriptions and think, "is this really describing one who outdid beauty in all human beings?" In fact, feminist scholars Athalya Brenner and Fiona Black go to great lengths to illustrate that this woman is not, in fact, beautiful. Brenner purports that 7:1–7 is merely a parody of a wasf, that the woman's thighs and vulva are viewed as beautiful, but her stomach and breasts are the objects of ridicule.[86] She surmises that the lover is actually poking fun of her jiggling belly and bouncing breasts as she dances. Further, Fiona Black describes the parodied wasf as part of the grotesque genre as grotesque allows for the "portrayal of things that might not comfortably be portrayed, such as the female figure in an erotic context."[87] And I would contend that it is *possible* that Brenner and Black are correct in assuming that the dancer is being teased for her pudgy body by her lover. However, I find it hard to believe that a lover would dote upon the dancer's feet, thighs (also plump), and vulva with complete admiration and quickly shift to ridicule her stomach and breasts. Perhaps these feminists

---

85. This translation of *One Thousand and One Nights* is taken from Brenner, *I Am . . . Biblical Women Tell Their Own Stories*, 165–66.

86. Brenner goes to great and somewhat convincing lengths to support her claim that this is a wasf parody. Her exegesis can be found in several books and articles: Brenner, *The Song of Songs*, "Come Back, Come Back the Shulamite," and *I Am . . . Biblical Women Tell Their Own Stories*.

87. Black, "Unlikely Bedfellows," 106–7.

are projecting our contemporary standards of beauty back throughout history onto this dancer. As illustrated in the wasf *One Thousand and One Nights*, voluptuous and curvy women were described as "beautiful," in fact as the "loveliest creature Allah had made." Furthermore, curvy and full-figured women are the norm in bellydance. In fact, one of the most frequently praised aspects of bellydance is its openness to women of all body types.[88] "Women sense the veneration for the female body which, unlike so many bodies on display (especially in the West), does not have to be thin or absurdly youthful. The focus on the hips [an area many women dislike most] allows women to reclaim and accept the site of that which marks us as female."[89] In fact, one of Egypt's premier bellydancers, Souhair Zaki, could be described in a similar manner as the Shulamite. Zaki's dance was described as follows: "[She] was the most celebrated dancer in Cairo, but she hadn't seen thirty in a while. Flesh clung heavily to her hips. Her abdomen bulged like a ripe pear. I had never seen traditional oriental dance before, but I recognized every movement. What she was doing . . . was what a woman's body *did*—the natural movements of sex and childbirth. The dance drew the eye to the hips and abdomen, the very center of the female body's womanliness."[90] Like the Shulamite, the damsel from *One Thousand and One Nights*, and Souhair Zaki, bellydance celebrates the female form, praising its curves and folds. "Rather than shunning and hiding her feminine form and the creative, mothering power that her body represents, the woman who wants to bellydance must embrace her body and its movements."[91] Quivering bellies, trembling thighs, shaking buttocks, and shuddering breasts are precisely the point. Contemporary American culture may not see the Shulamite's dancing body as beautiful, but her lover certainly did.

And perhaps this is precisely what we are to glean from the sexy words of Song of Songs 7:1–4. Perhaps the lesson returns to us with the Shulamite's dancing curves. Perhaps the holy does, indeed, dwell within our bodies—our sexual, growing, dancing, aching, aging, gendered, moving bodies. We do not hear God's name spoken throughout the canticle and we wonder if God is present at all. But perhaps God's presence in manifest the Shulamite's dancing body, in our dancing bodies. Perhaps the Shulamite's curved thighs

88. Crosby, "The Goddess Dances," 174.

89. Ibid.

90. Ibid.

91. Coluccia et al., *Belly Dancing*, 7.

can remind us to "love our flesh."[92] Maybe this dancer's quivering belly can teach us to "love our bodies regardless."[93] The bellydance in the Song of Songs helps us recall that our bodies were created as "good"—not depraved, less-than, or despised by God—but "good." As all bellydance serve to affirm women's sexuality, to aid in childbirth, to connect to the goddess within, perhaps we can reclaim the ancient and sacred roots of bellydance. As the lover gazes upon the dancing Shulamite with complete adoration and delight, so too does God gaze upon each of our dancing bodies, delighted and in awe. Passionate lovers embrace and dance together as an affirmation that this passionate love must be a part of our worshiping lives. Our passionate bodies are "crafted by artist hands," beautiful, beloved, and a dancing place for undulating the holy.

How the Shulamite's Dance Can Revolutionize Worship Today

The Shulamite's dance from Song of Songs 7 is a stirring reminder that worship must not simply affirm the body, but truly meaningful worship must also provocatively affirm passionate love. As the Shulamite's lover dotes upon her dancing body, so too, must worship leaders dote upon the body of Christ. This entails affirming the physical body, sexuality, and passion within the body of Christ.

Dance is a primary way of affirming the physical body. Moving, dancing, and embodying prayers is a key way to revolutionize the worship of congregations who are typically static or seated throughout most of the worship hour. Proclaiming the Word provides opportunities to speak positively of the body and the flesh rather than dualistically creating a negative opposition between spirit and body. Redeeming the body through physical touch, passing the peace, the kiss of peace, or the laying on of hands are also prime opportunities for affirming the physical body. Teaching simple circle dances, where congregants move hand-in-hand with their faith community is both a physical and embodied way of affirming the body. These simple circle dances also help many congregants realize that they, too, can be dancers. Finally, solo or ensemble dances performed by professional or lay dancers that emphasize the entire body—not simply feet and hands, but

92. "Love your flesh" here refers to Toni Morrison's plea manifest in the monologue of Baby Suggs, holy, in her novel, *Beloved*.

93. I am borrowing from Alice Walker's sentiments describing womanist's call to love herself: regardless.

also the movement and nuances of the torso, hips, and back—affirm the body in a way that is not typical in much contemporary worship.

This type of holistic dancing is also a way to affirm sexuality. Typically, many so-called liturgical dancers minimize the hips, torso, or back in their dancing, often hiding them behind loose garments that are difficult for good dancers to move in. Acknowledging and embodying every part of the body reminds congregants that the entire sexual body is a part of God's good creation. Subverting patriarchal gender stereotypes in dance can also affirm passionate love and sexuality. For example, a woman can dance the role of Christ or God. A committed, loving relationship could be performed in a dance between persons of the same gender. Finally, choreography that does not always place God up in the heavens, but in the nexus of the body, dwelling in the heart or belly, can also affirm the sexual body.

A third way the Shulamite's dance can inspire and transform worship is by affirming passion. Passion holds a precarious role in Christian worship. On the one hand it is often shunned as negative because of its association with the carnal, lustful, or fleshly. On the other hand, passion is affirmed during Holy Week as countless Christians remember the passion of Christ. In this instance, passion refers to the outpouring of love so deep that it leads to death on a cross. However, in the case of the dancing Shulamite, the sexual body is affirmed in a way that causes these two connotations of passion to merge. Passionate love is affirmed, not only in the crucifixion, but also in the deep, abiding love of the Shulamite's lover, doting upon her every curve. This passionate love is, indeed, holy. Mutually respectful, loving relationships, likewise, are holy and in need of affirmation. Most committed lovers are quick to express a willingness to live and die for the other in a manner similar to passion shared by Christ. This willingness, this unending and passionate love, must be reclaimed and redeemed in contemporary worship.

In order for the worshiping church to survive and thrive, it must affirm passionate love. The Shulamite's dance is a prime example and inspiration of such passionate love. By preaching her story, singing her praises, and embodying her sensual dance, we too, may avow passionate love in our worship. We, too, can revolutionize worship by affirming passionate love in our bodies, words, and dances.

CHAPTER 6

Judith's Dance: Subversion

Judith 15:12–13

Violence dismembered; malice beheaded
Victory drips from a drunken head
Seduction fails; a widow prays   ⁕
Beauty dances toward liberation and freedom

Beautiful. Wise. Courageous. Faithful. Subversive. Liberator. Dancer. There is no other woman in all of Scripture quite like Judith. A stunning and faithful widow delivers Israel by beheading the enemy after a moment of prayer. All the women of Israel celebrate their newfound freedom by dancing in her honor. Judith responds by leading them in song and dance. Gender, dancing, sexuality, seduction, and music merge in a subverted liturgical event inaugurated by a pious woman. In order to understand the efficacy of Judith's dance and how it may revolutionize worship today, it is first imperative to recount the intrigue of her deliverance of Israel.

The book of Judith joins Esther, Ruth, and Suzanna as one of the few books to bear the name of a woman as its title. This signals, perhaps, that the story found within is unique, subversive, and somehow different than the many stories caught in the torrents of patriarchy found elsewhere in Scripture. The first seven chapters of Judith describe the military onslaught of the Assyrian general Holofernes who wishes to conquer Judith's city of Bethulia in honor of his lord, Nebuchadnezzar. In addition to the siege, Bethulia has suffered from an extensive and prolonged drought. The elders are in despair. They plead with God to intervene, but in a moment of thirsty panic, determine that they will surrender to Holofernes if God does not deliver them within five days. This surrender would not only admit militaristic defeat; it would also imply that Nebuchadnezzar is mightier than YHWH.

The crux of the narrative shifts in chapter 8 when our beloved dancing widow enters the scene. Israel is ready to surrender when Judith leaves the mourning of her widowhood behind to confront the elders. Judith upbraids them for their cowardice, condemning their lack of faith in God, and announces a secret plan to save her people. After sending the elders away to pray, Judith prays a long and ardent prayer, imploring God to empower and strengthen her. After much prayer, Judith begins the beautification process. Bathing, anointing her body with oils, and dressing in her finest clothing and jewelry partner with the sincerity of her prayers to prepare her for battle. Judith and her female maid gather a bag of festival foods and depart to find Holofernes, intent on delivering Israel and remaining faithful to YHWH. With a tiara on her head, the pious widow sets out to redeem her people.

The moment Judith enters the Assyrian camp, the soldiers are so astonished by her beauty that they direct her immediately to Holofernes' tent, saying, "Who could despise a people having women look like this?" (Jdt 10:19). They appear dumbfounded by her beauty, unable to question her intentions, agency, or power; they see her as nothing more than a beautiful face. As she enters Holofernes' tent, Judith prostrates herself and lies, pledging her loyalty to Nebuchadnezzar. Overcome with her beauty and declared loyalty, Holofernes invites Judith to dine and drink with him, but she refuses, explaining that she must keep her dietary rules and remain faithful to her nightly time of prayer. For three days Judith sleeps in a tent beside Holofernes, leaving each evening for prayer.

On the third evening, Holofernes invites Judith to a banquet. Again, after prayer and a beautification process, Judith joins Holofernes and he is overtaken by her beauty. Intent on seducing her, Holofernes begins an evening of intense drinking. He drank more in that one evening than he had ever drank. Left alone in the tent with a very drunk Holofernes, Judith prays for strength and then chops Holofernes' head off with his own sword. She calls upon her beloved maid to bring her the bag used for carrying ritual foods and places the severed head inside. As the two women leave the campground with the bag, none of the Assyrian warriors suspect any foul play because the two women have faithfully left camp each evening for prayer.

Upon their return to Bethulia, Judith calls the Israelites to prayer and shows them Holofernes' severed head. She proclaims, "Praise God! The Lord has struck him down by hands of a woman!" (Jdt 13:16). The Israelite army then takes advantage of the now leaderless Assyrians. After defeating the Assyrians and ensuring their victory, the women of Israel gather to see Judith. As women have greeted and blessed victorious warriors after battle throughout all of ancient Israel, so too do these women bless Judith and dance in her honor. Then Judith distributes branches and garlands among the women and leads them in song and dance. The men follow her lead. It is this surprising, subversive, and celebratory dance that has the potential to revolutionize worship today.

In order to understand more fully why Judith's dance teaches us about the power of subversion, it is first imperative to examine Judith's character and how it is subverted in ways that make her an alternative leader. This examination will lead us to the subversive power embedded in the ritual of her dance.

Judith's Virtuous Character

It is Judith's virtuosity that enables her subversive power. So, let us begin with the virtues that describe her character. The text depicts her as a pious, beautiful, wise, faithful, brave, wealthy widow. Rarely in Scripture are women afforded these seemingly divergent descriptions because biblical women are often portrayed as one dimensional characters. They can beautiful, but their faithfulness or piety may be questioned. They may be wise and filled with faith, but their appearance is never mentioned or it is asexualized. Judith is unique in that she is beautiful *and* faithful, pious *and* wise, a widow *and* wealthy, a woman *and* a warrior. A seminal scholar of the Book of Judith, Toni Craven, elaborates further, saying, "Judith is the archetype of the unconventional, beautiful, brainy woman for whom militarism, faulty theology, foolish vows, apostasy, terrorism, persecution, widowhood, sex, murder and even death hold no fear."[1]

What is more, Judith's faith stands in stark contrast with the other characters throughout the book. Unlike the leaders of Bethulia, she does not pray and then give up. She prays and then puts her prayers to action, having faith that God will protect her and her people. She does not manipulate God by putting a time limit on the amount of time her prayers must

1. Craven, "The Book of Judith," 187.

be answered. Further, the text offers no divine response or guarantee that Judith's prayer shall be fulfilled. Unlike the Assyrians, she does not make threats. Interestingly, all of the foils in the text, those whose characters contrast with that of Judith, are male. In fact, with the exception of her female maid and the women who dance in her honor at the end of the story, every character in the book is male except for Judith. Rarely is there a biblical tale where every male lacks faith, but a woman is filled with faith. Moreover, Judith also assumes the role of a man in leadership by securing military victory and leading in ritual. So, the men in the text lack faith, fail to lead in battle, and do not lead in ritual. Instead, the pious widow must assume all of these leadership roles at once.

Both Judith's name and character represent the Jewish community. Her name literally means "Jewess" and she embodies the underdog status of the Israelite people. They are the oppressed, attacked, marginalized "others" who are under siege by the Assyrians. Amy Jill-Levine elaborates further: "Judith the character is usually identified as a representation of or a metaphor for the community of faith. Although her name, widowhood, chastity, beauty and righteousness suggest the traditional representation of Israel, the text's association of these traits with an independent woman and with sexuality subverts the metaphoric connection between character and androcentrically determined community."[2]

Judith's character typifies what it means to be a faithful, dedicated Jew who trusts in God even when times are difficult. Even as she grieves the death of her husband, she establishes agency for herself as an independent woman, while also trusting God's deliverance when her religious leaders fail to trust. In the face of their disbelief, Judith believes. Craven continues further, "In the face of a life-threatening situation, her people are ready to be unfaithful. By contrast, Judith adopts the radical stance that to God alone belongs the decision regarding their survival."[3]

So, it is clear that Judith's character is one of piety, virtuosity, and faith. She is also an autonomous woman. Amy-Jill Levine contends that "Judith had to be a widow—that is, sexually experienced but unattached—in order for her to carry out her plan."[4] In these ways, Judith remains chaste in the midst of drunken seduction. She remains unattached in the midst of her extreme beauty. Even with multiple male suitors vying for Judith's hand, she

2. Levine, "Sacrifice and Salvation," 208.
3. Craven, "Artistry and Faith," 3.
4. Levine, "Sacrifice and Salvation," 213.

remains single and lives with her female maid in widowhood. Moreover, the Hebrew Bible is replete with admonitions to take care of the poor, the orphan, and the widow. The cries of the prophets to protect widows are enumerable. Yet, Judith is a widow who does not need protection. Instead, Judith—the pious widow— protects her people. Even though she is noted as remarkably attractive throughout the text, she is not defined by her relationship to a man, but instead by her faithfulness, piety, and wisdom. She is unequivocally depicted as adhering to every positive virtue: wise, faithful, brave, pious, beautiful, and devout.

Subverting Judith's Character

It is Judith's irreproachable character that validates her subversive power. She subverts traditional roles in three primary ways: in her widowhood, in her gender, and as a warrior. Craven begins this subversive conversation; her words are worth recounting at length:

> The story of Judith's triumph is one of cultural paradox. In a clearly male dominated society, one in which women gather around males for direction (7:23ff.) only to be sent home with the children (7:32), Judith unexpectedly calls male rulers to accountability (8:11). A woman of habitual prayer (8:4–6), she ignores Uzziah's counsel to pray for rain (8:31). A woman of financial substance, she entrusts the running of her household to another female (8:10). One of Judith's final acts before her death at one hundred five years of age is to free this faithful female servant who had accompanied her to the Assyrian camp (16:23).[5]

First, let us consider how Judith subverts traditional understanding of what it means to be a widow. According to Amy Jill-Levine, Judith conforms to traditional understandings of Israel as a woman in mourning in that both she and Bethulia are literally or metaphorically draped in sackcloths. However, she subverts the traditional understanding of widowhood in other ways. "Judith's particular representation—her status, rhetoric, wealth, beauty and even her genealogy—aborts the metaphor. This widow is hardly the forlorn female in need of male protection."[6] She functions on her own financially, asserting both emotional and economic independence from men. As noted previously, she also does not require the protection of men

5. Craven, "Artistry and Faith," 94.
6. Levine, "Sacrifice and Salvation," 212.

or religious leaders (also men) as a widow, but instead protects them. The wealth of her widowhood sets her further outside the bounds of traditional female roles. She is not a mother or wife and she needs no man to support her livelihood. Instead, she has both agency and autonomy, something many women in Scripture are rarely afforded.

Since Judith's widowhood is part of her gendered and sexual characterization, this moves naturally into examining how she subverted traditional understandings of gender and sexuality. Primary in examining how Judith subverts gender and sexuality is Deborah Sawyer's "Dressing Up/Dressing Down: Power, Performance and Identity in the Book of Judith."[7] Sawyer claims that "the story of Judith is a clear illustration of gender subversion in the ancient world"[8] because the author of Judith "employs gender as an elusive category rather than one that is split down its middle and staked at two polarities."[9] Judith does not rely on a man for her identity or financial livelihood. She does not adhere to the role of the quiet wife or pious woman who only listens to the authoritative voice of male religious leaders. Instead, she lives independently with another female, undermining both traditional and heteronormative assumptions of what constitute a family. Instead, she lives with her maid as a female companion and condemns the unfaithful voices of the male religious leaders in the story. Sawyer elaborates further:

> In undermining the normative dualisms of conventional gender behavior, and by offering us cold-blooded murder as an act of redemption, the author of the book of Judith authenticates divine omniscience. The author uses the device of unconventionality to support the readers' expectations, but his purpose is not ultimately anarchic. In biblical terms this is a conventional use of the female hero—one that allows God to act in the most unexpected fashion.[10]

What is more, all of the men in the Book of Judith are essentially emasculated: her husband, Mannasah, by virtue of his unheroic death, Holofernes by virtue of his decapitation (read castration), and the male leaders of Bethulia by virtue of their unfaithfulness.[11] Not only are these men emasculated by

---

7. Sawyer, "Dressing Up/Dressing Down."

8. Ibid., 25.

9. Ibid., 23–24

10. Ibid., 25.

11. For more on the relationship between decapitation and castration see Dundes, "Comment on Narrative Structures in the Book of Judith," 28–29.

the author, but "by the hands of a woman," that is Judith, the pious widow and warrior.

Judith's undermining of traditional understandings of widowhood, gender, and sexuality usher in the possibility for her to become a warrior. Craven highlights that the "lies" Judith tells in prayer and battle lead to the redemption of her people.[12] In both Judith 9:10 and 13, she asks God to make her a good liar. Additionally, she successfully uses deceit to preserve her community. "Paradoxically, the congruence of her actions and prayer challenges other more devastating lies in the book: specifically those of the Jewish community, and most notably Uzziah and Holofernes."[13]

Clad in her finest jewels, clothing, and a tiara, she prays devoutly, and then marches toward the Assyrian camp for battle. It is in this "disguise as the *femme fatale* that Judith will redeem Israel."[14] It is her beauty that dumb-founds the Assyrian warriors who point her in the direction of Holofernes. It is her beauty that leads Holofernes to try and seduce her and become limp with drunkenness. And it is when she is draped with her most beautiful clothing and jewels that she severs Holofernes' drunken head. And she does so without forsaking her chastity. Her beauty and piety collide to elude any possible questioning from the Assyrian warriors as she leaves camp with the blood of their general's head staining her food bag. She becomes the mighty warrior and is greeted accordingly. In fact, in the same manner in which ancient Israelite women greet victorious *men* upon their return from battle, so the women greet Judith with songs and dances in her honor. In these ways, Judith subverts traditional understandings of widowhood, gender, sexuality, and battle to become the mighty warrior who dances in the garments of a queen, the head of her enemy dangling from her jeweled hands, hands that were previously clasped in pious prayer. Her speech and actions parody the patriarchal gender codes, while her feminine appearance adds to the subversive power of her actions . . . in prayer, in battle, in song, and in dance.

Judith's Subversive Dance

All the women of Israel gathered to see her; and they blessed her and danced in her honor.

---

12. Craven, "Women Who Lied for the Faith."

13. Ibid., 13.

14. Sawyer, "Dressing Up/Dressing Down," 28.

She took branches in her hands and distributed them to the women around her, and she and the other women crowned themselves with garlands of olive leaves.

At the head of all the people, she led the women in dance . . .[15]

Judith's ultimate subversive power lies in her role as ritual leader and dancer. Her subversions of what it means to be a widow, woman, and warrior all pave the way for her role as liturgist. In fact, Jan Willem Van Henten asserts that Judith is an alternative leader in every sense, even noting that the Book of Judith may have been penned by a female (F):

> [An] indication of a possible F voice seems to be the departure from the traditional pattern of men who act as warriors and liberators, and women who sing the song of victory. The Hebrew Bible contains several specimens of such a victory song or references to it (Exod. 15:20–21; Judg 11:34; 1 Sam. 18:6–7). Judith 15–16 corresponds to them, but again it is the deviation from the usual pattern which gives reason to assume a narrative F voice . . . In the book of Judith . . . all the women from Israel come together, start dancing and singing with timbrels, praising the victor . . . It looks like a reversal of gender roles . . . There is a possibility that they were originally composed as a parody of male leadership for a female audience."[16]

Except in the cases of dance that we have examined throughout this text, women were rarely afforded opportunities for ritual leadership. So, Judith joins Miriam, Jephthah's daughter, and the Shulamite in the annals of history as some of the few female ritual leaders. It is worth noting that their voices, proclamations, or prayers were not what gave these women ritual authority. Rather, it was their songs and dances that provided them with liturgical agency. Judith's dance was the culmination of her subversive power and it resulted in her leading a liturgical event.

In fact, Toni Craven asserts that Judith's song and dance parallels the Song of the Sea from Exodus 15.[17] It is in a moment of redemption, freedom, and liberation that Judith offers up a celebratory song and dance, much like Miriam. In these ways, Judith's dance seems merely a celebration. In context, however, the subversive power of Judith's character transforms

---

15. Jdt 15:12–13.

16. Van Henten, "Judith as Alternative Leader," 251–52.

17. Craven, "Artistry and Faith," 10.

the dance. It is not through the deliverance brought on by the acts of a brother that Judith begins to dance and sing. In this way, her ritual leadership is different than Miriam's. It is not even through the deliverance of God that Judith begins to dance and sing. In this way, she is also different than Miriam. Both dances celebrate liberation and freedom, to be sure, but the exodus event is at the hand of God, while the people of Bethulia are delivered through the hands of a woman. Judith's actions give her liturgical agency. The agency of this dancing widow then subverts traditional understandings of victory dances.

Furthermore, Judith's dance is subverted in even more communal ways. The dance begins, not based on the rhythmic movement of Judith, but of the women who greet her upon her return to Bethulia. As noted earlier, the traditional dance of greeting is subverted. As other Israelite women exit their homes to greet *men* upon their victorious return of battle, so the women of Bethulia exit their homes to greet Judith with dances and song. She becomes both warrior and ritual leader, both positions traditionally reserved for men. The dancing women of Bethulia are the prelude to the liturgical event whose wise leader subverts the ritual at every turn. The dancing widow—Judith, the subverted ritual leader—now includes those previously excluded from ritual performativity in the dance. Amy Jill-Levine contends further:

> Upon her return, the seeds of Judith's threat begin to flower in Israel. By her actions and by her presence, she offers those previously marginal to or excluded from the power base—Jewish women, Achior the Gentile, the maidservant—roles in society and cult . . . Some [women] even danced in her honor. In turn, she distributes branches to her companions. These women, who then "crowned themselves with olive wreaths," reveal their transformation into active agents. Last, Judith leads "all the women" while "every man" followed them.[18]

Judith leads the women, and the women lead the men. The men follow. The patriarchal order is reversed. And those who had never had an opportunity to lead or participate in traditional ritual events began to dance, sing, dress up, and lead. In these ways, Judith's dance—the culmination of all of her subversive activities—turns traditional ritual on its head. Men follow. Women lead. Religious leaders are in the wrong. The pious widow is in the right. Songs and dances worship the God of liberation. And those who have

18. Levine, "Sacrifice and Salvation," 218.

never experienced ritual leadership—women, Gentiles, widows, servants—step into the dancing shoes of ritual authority. And it is all because one beautiful widow dared to challenge the status quo. Her courageous dance steps subverted ritual leadership in Bethulia. And Judith's dance steps have the power to subversively revolutionize worship today.

How Judith's Dance Can Revolutionize Worship Today

The subversive power of Judith's dance has the potential to revolutionize worship today. Throughout this book, I have suggested a variety of ways in which the body and dance can be incorporated more fully into worship. These examples continue to ring true when embodying the subversive potential of Judith's dance in liturgy. In fact, I would contend that in most churches, incorporating dance and movement is a subversive act in and of itself simply because so many churches remain static, seated, and stationary during worship. When worshipers neglect their bodies and only worship with their hearts, heads, or voices, incorporating the simple movement of arms, legs, and torso is, indeed, a subversive act. But I would like to make more specific suggestions for how to subvert liturgy in creative and surprising ways, only some of which involve dance or movement.

A primary way one may use subversion to revolutionize worship is to utilize the talents and leadership of any people otherwise excluded from liturgical authority due to denominational or church polity. In some churches this may be women. In others it may be persons with developmental disabilities.[19] In many, it may be LGBTQ persons. Any church that intentionally or unintentionally excludes the voices of people from these beloved communities likely functions in ways similar to the elders of Bethulia. It takes the brave acts of individuals like Judith to subvert these exclusive regulations. So, upbraid the authoritative structures that lack the faith to bravely include diverse people called of God into leadership because their theologies or polities are too limited, constrained, or exclusive. When authoritative powers are so bound to tradition that they exclude voices and bodies God has lovingly created, unbind them with acts of courage like Judith. "Queer" liturgy[20] in ways that include the oppressed

19. For more on incorporating persons with disabilities into worship see Patterson, "Redeemed Bodies," 123–43.

20. For more on the concept of queering liturgy, see chapter 2 of Fennema's "Falling All Around Me."

and marginalized in positions of leadership.[21] The dances, songs, prayers, and proclamations of LGBTQ persons have the potential to subvert and revolutionize worship in ways that are powerful, meaningful, and libratory, much like Judith's dance. What might worship look like through their eyes, through their perspective?

In addition to incorporating persons otherwise excluded from liturgical leadership as a way to subversively revolutionize worship, churches may also invite unexpected people to lead worship. For example, having children take on "adult" leadership positions by serving communion or preaching would certainly subvert the status quo. In the same way that Judith—an individual traditionally excluded from ritual leadership—passed out garlands to the women, so too could children pass garlands to worshipers or drape stoles over the clergy. It would be even more powerful if the children also wore stoles or other garments of ecclesial authority, embodying the concept of the priesthood of all believers. Doing so while the congregation sings the spiritual, "I Got a Robe, You Got a Robe, All God's Children Got a Robe" would prove liberating, equalizing, and powerfully subversive.

Subverting traditional gender constructions by having women read the parts of God, Jesus, Moses, Abraham, or other traditionally male figures in Scripture also proves provocatively powerful. I recall inviting a female congregant in her early sixties to read the part of Jesus in a text while two men read the narrator and disciple roles. While she only spoke two pithy lines, this woman was moved to tears. When I later asked why she was so moved, she explained that the sheer thought of Jesus being a woman like her was so powerful, so liberating, that she could not stop her weeping. Worship was subversively revolutionized simply by asking this woman to read the words of Jesus from Scripture that are most often assigned to men.

Preaching from the pew rather than the pulpit, equalizing the space by rearranging chairs into a circle, or moving the clergy or choir out of a lifted chancel area and onto level ground with the congregation are all ways to subvert traditional understandings of space, power, hierarchy, and authority. Judith's dance subverted traditional liturgical leadership because she dared to step into the space reserved for male leadership. It was not only her gender, but the gendered space that needed subverting. This is also true in worship today. Examine your worship space. Are only particular people permitted in particular places? If so, why? Might you subvert, shift,

21. For more on how to incorporate the subversive topics of sexuality, gender, or the body into worship see Yarber, *The Gendered Pulpit*.

or reverse these spaces in ways that would lead toward an equalization of roles, a leveling of leadership possibilities, and the opportunity for the empowerment of persons otherwise excluded from spaces of authority. While it may appear like a small step, inviting someone who is from a group that it is traditionally excluded to stand behind the pulpit can subvert exclusive worshiping patterns. These subversive acts—no matter how small—have the potential to revolutionize worship today.

Judith's dance revolutionized worship by including a dancing widow in the space of ritual authority. Her act of courage led to the inclusion of others previously excluded from ritual leadership. Who might you include to subvert the status quo? How will you subvert oppressive patterns of worship by embodying subversion like Judith?

CHAPTER 7

Salome's Dance: Innocence

Mark 6:17–29 and Matthew 14:3–11

But an opportunity came when Herod on his birthday gave a banquet for his courtiers and officers and for the leaders of Galilee. When his daughter Herodias came in and danced, she pleased Herod and his guests; and the king said to the girl, "Ask me for whatever you wish, and I will give it." And he solemnly swore to her, "Whatever you ask me, I will give you, even half of my kingdom." She went out and said to her mother, "What should I ask for?" She replied, "The head of John the baptizer."

—MARK 6:21–24

The scene is a seminary classroom. The topic takes a turn and the dance of Salome becomes the subject of great debate. When a female student notes that Salome was a young child and that her reputation has been scandalized by patriarchal interpreters and artists who turn her innocent dance steps into sultry seduction, a male student responds with antagonistic vigor. "Salome was a slut. She might as well have had a stripper pole in the middle of the room when she danced," he balks. Responding to this student's grave misunderstanding—and all those who share his opinion of Salome—is the aim of this chapter.

If you carefully read Mark 6:17–29 and Matthew 14:3–11, you may wonder why this chapter is dedicated to someone named Salome. There was no mention of anyone named Salome in the text. Rather, in the Markan text both the dancing daughter and her mother are named Herodias. In Matthew's text, the daughter is nameless. It was not until later that Flavius

Josephus, a Jewish historian, named her Salome, though he never stated that she was guilty for the beheading of John the Baptist.[1] Because of the way artists, playwrights, choreographers, and filmmakers have presented this story, however, the dance of Salome has been scandalized and misinterpreted for centuries. In order to understand how her dance might revolutionize worship today, we must first plough through this history of misunderstanding. Recounting this history will lead us back to the text to compare the two gospels accounts of her dance. Finally, after reviewing artistic misrepresentations and exegeting the texts, I will conclude by explaining how Salome's dance can revolutionize worship today.

Scandalizing Salome

Since Josephus made up her name, interpreters have gone crazy with blame, ruining the poor little girl's reputation. The more prominent John the Baptist became in history, the more infamous Salome became. This is reflected in the arts, as well. In fact, Diane Apostolos-Cappadona contends that by the medieval period "Salome" and her mother fused into one person and that by the nineteenth century they collided to form the ultimate femme fatale.[2]

In 1462 we have Gozzoli's rendering of Salome, which shows the dance of an innocent child doing gymnastics and twirling the way many little children do when given the spotlight. Perhaps Gozzoli translated Greek in addition to producing famous paintings, because it is clear that the word used to described "Salome" is *thygatros*, which means "little daughter." I will examine these words choices in more detail soon. Based solely on what the text says, and even these early artistic renderings, it is obvious that this scripture is about a little girl dancing for play and fun and then being taken advantage of by a conniving mother and uncle; I will return to these assertions when exegeting the text, though. It is worth noting that many medieval and early Renaissance artists depict a dancing girl that is closer to the text. She is young, seemingly asexual, and she dances playfully and acrobatically. This dancing girl reflects the historical role of liturgical dance in the church in that it is still practiced regularly. Because the church is dancing in worship, so too is Salome in artistic renderings.

---

1. Apostolos-Cappadona, "Scriptural Women Who Danced," 98.
2. Ibid., 100.

As the role of dance begins to decline, however, a profound shift occurs in the high Renaissance and baroque periods, when "the image of Salome is transformed in Western art into a vehicle for depicting female beauty. She becomes slowly disassociated from the narrative of the scriptural story."[3] In the art of Titian, Sebastiano del Piombo, and Guido Reni, Salome is no longer depicted as an innocent dancing girl but instead as a young beauty whose porcelain skin and ornately proper dress stands in stark contrast to the bloody severed head on the platter she holds. When the church dances less, the artists portraying Salome no longer depict a dancing girl. What is more, the depiction of Salome clings less and less to the biblical text.

With the development of the femme fatale in nineteenth and twentieth century art, film, and literature, Salome's story was quickly exaggerated. Gustave Moreau painted over one hundred images of Salome in the 1870s, all illustrating a seductive woman in gauzy fabric.[4] She is a woman in slinky garb, her disheveled hair piled upon her head like that of a courtesan, parts of her body previously hidden are now exposed and awaiting a lusty gaze. Then Oscar Wilde wrote his infamous play, *Salome*, in 1894, and it is clear that he never bothered to even read the accounts from the Gospels because his play includes an adult Salome flirting with John the Baptist, stripping down to a dance of seven veils, and then kissing the severed head on a bloody platter. Toni Bentley describes the reputation-altering power of Wilde's play: "Forever altering her legend, Wilde gave Salome the Dance of the Seven Veils. In so doing he gave her—and her sisters-to-be—room to maneuver, creating a movement larger in scale, surely, than even he might have imagined. Instead of a gymnastic, circus dance on her hands, or a gleeful maiden dance with a ribboned tambourine as in her medieval renditions, Wilde assigned Salome nothing more—or less—than a striptease."[5] Performing artists subsequently went wild (pun intended) with the story. Richard Strauss composed an opera based on Wilde's play, emphasizing the lascivious dance of the seven veils and concluding with "the dramatic ending in which Salome is crushed to death by Herod's soldiers as she kisses the lips of the decapitated head of John the Baptist."[6] Loie Fuller and Maude

---

3. Ibid., 101.
4. Ibid., 102.
5. Bentley, *Sisters of Salome*, 30.
6. Apostolos-Cappadona, "Scriptural Women Who Danced," 104

Allan choreographed dances that are little more than a striptease as they embody the "dance of seven veils."[7]

Entire volumes are dedicated to reviewing the way Salome was portrayed in choreography, film, visual art, and theatre. Toni Bentley's *Sisters of Salome* details the history of "Salomania" and includes in-depth research about the four most scandalous women who personified Salome and performed her "seductive" dance.[8] Bentley beautifully recounts the revealing of Sidonie Gabrielle Colette's breast as she describes the way this French novelist portrayed Salome's dance. She details Maud Allan's danced depiction of Salome and how this dance eventually led her to be "accused" of lesbianism and brought to trial. These accusations, trial, and dance were memorialized as the "cult of the clitoris." Bentley tells the story of Mata Hari's nude Salome dance, along with how Ida Rubinstein embodied Salome for Russian audiences. The dances and stories of these four women are filled with intrigue, drama, steamy sex, and empowered sensuality. Bentley's accounts are factual, fascinating, and reveal previously unheard history involving modern depictions of Salome. Her work is truly intriguing. Not once, however, is Salome's actual story recounted. Never do we read the biblical text in these myriad modern renditions of the dancing daughter. I say this not to indict Bentley's book; it is thoughtful, critical, and interesting. I say this because modern artistic interpretations have moved so far from the actual biblical text that they have maligned our ability to interpret the text itself. Amidst it all, a little girl's reputation is destroyed and dance is demonized as nothing more than an agent of seduction and slander. In these ways, popular culture impacts our understanding of Salome's dance even more than the Bible does.

If we chalk the plays, the opera, the paintings, and the choreography up to extreme poetic licensing, then perhaps we can return to the heart of the text. And we'll see the story of a little girl who was asked to dance by a family member at a party. I have many such memories from my own childhood as I cried "Watch me! Watch me!" to parents, aunts, uncles, and grandparents while I leapt and twirled, filled with the childlike innocence that adults often forget when it comes to worship. I am convinced that Salome's dance was no different.

7. For an extended list and descriptions of Salome choreography, see Manor, *The Gospel According to Dance*, 56–72.

8. Bentley, *Sisters of Salome*.

Perhaps that male seminary student who attacked Salome with such slander, deeming the little child a "slut" in need of a "stripper pole," has paid more attention to the visual art, choreography, film, and theater that depicted this dancing daughter rather than reading, translating, and exegeting the text for himself. It is for these very reasons that I now turn to the texts of Matthew and Mark in search of the real Salome's dance.

Salome as a Dancing Daughter in Matthew and Mark

[Dancing] may evince a holy excitement, as when David danced before the ark. His dancing would be the hilarious stepping of a soul full of holy triumph . . . The dancing of Salome was of another kind. The dancing of the ball-room is a pernicious invention to excite criminal passion. It has often led to the sacrifice of chastity, and to murder afterwards to conceal shame . . . Christian mothers who send their daughters to the dancing-school should remember the mother of Salome.[9]

As the above quote indicates, even biblical interpreters are not immune to scandalizing the dancing daughter in Matthew and Mark. In fact, interpreting Salome as an evil temptress is relatively commonplace. Our task is to wade through the swirling waters of patriarchy that cloud our exegetical vision to see what the true nature of Salome's dance was. Was it the innocent dance of a young child or the seductive dance of a bloodthirsty woman? Is it possible that her dance falls into neither of these binaries but instead exists between the oppositional polarities? In order to answer these questions, I will expound upon the differences between the accounts in Matthew and Mark, examine key words in the text, explore the historicity of the narrative, and detail the role of gender in the text. Each of these elements will lead us to a better understanding of Salome's dance.

The two gospel accounts that include Salome's dance are Mark 6:17–29 and Matthew 14:3–11. The Gospel of Luke mentions the beheading of John the Baptist but includes no context, and the tale is left unrecorded in the Gospel of John. While there are a variety of differences in the accounts, there are only a few that are directly related to understanding Salome's dance. These two primary differences are who desires the death of John the Baptist and who the dancing daughter is. In the Gospel of Mark, Herodias wants John killed, whereas Matthew's shorter account indicates that it is

9. Spence and Excell, *The Pulpit Commentary*, 84.

Herod who wants the Baptist beheaded.[10] According to Caroline Vander Stichele, the most striking difference between the gospels is their portrayal of Herod's attitude toward John. She elaborating, saying:

> In both gospels Herod puts John in prison "because of Herodias."
> Next we read in Mark that Herodias wanted to kill him, but that
> she could not because Herod feared John (verses 19–20a). In Mat-
> thew, however, Herod and not Herodias wants to kill John. More-
> over, Herod fears the people not John "because they regarded him
> as a prophet" (Matthew 14:5). In Mark, on the contrary, Herod's
> attitude towards John is in fact remarkably positive. He considers
> John as "a righteous and holy man" and "he liked to listen to him"
> (verse 20): this has no parallel in Matthew.[11]

Consequently, the character of Herodias is culpable in both accounts, while Herod shares the blame only in Matthew. This is an important distinction since Herodias and her dancing daughter are often conflated into one scandalous female character. It is worth noting, however, that the daughter shares little blame according to either text. She follows her mother's orders. She is obedient. While the desires of Herodias and Herod are explicitly named, the daughter's are not.

Mark describes her as "his daughter, Herodias," thereby implying that she is the daughter of Antipas in 6:22. However, later in Mark, in verses 24 and 29, she is described as the daughter of Herodias, in addition to calling the dancing daughter Herodias. Therefore, Mark's account makes it is unclear whether the daughter and mother are both named Herodias, whether the daughter belongs only to Herodias, or whether she is daughter of Herod and Herodias. Matthew's account attempts to correct Mark 6:22 by consistently identifying the dancing girl as the daughter of Herodias in 14:6, 8, and 11. Gillman contends that "from very early in the literature of Christianity this dancing daughter of Herodias was assumed to have been the child of her first marriage, Salome, as her name is given by Josephus."[12] While Matthew and Mark disagree—at least in part—on whether she was the shared daughter of Herod and Herodias, the dancing daughter receives very little attention or description in either text. She appears. She dances. She is obedient to her mother's request. Descriptions of her dance or her intentions are missing altogether in both accounts.

---

10. Gillman, *Herodias*, 52.

11. Vander Stichele, "Murderous Mother, Ditto Daughter."

12. Gillman, *Herodias*, 54–55.

The two gospels also diverge on the words used for daughter. The accounts do not disagree on the word used for daughter, but both accounts utilize two different words for daughter: *thygatros*, which literally means "little daughter" and *korasion*, which is a bit more complicated to translate. Interestingly, when the daughter is first introduced in both gospels she is called *thygatros* or "little daughter." There are ostensibly no sexual connotations with this word. So, as the scene opens in both accounts, we are introduced to a little daughter. *After* she dances, there is another word used and it is the topic of endless debate among scholars who want to place Salome into one of two dichotomous categories: innocent child or beautiful temptress. This word is *korasion*. *Korasion* is the diminutive of *korē*, "a girl." Florence Gillman contends that *korē* also "denotes the pupil of an eye or the 'apple' of an eye. *Korasion* should be translated 'little girl,' however, since Greek popular speech of this period did not necessarily use diminutives in a diminutive sense. This term could designate a small child, but most often it denotes a young girl at or near marriageable age."[13] The notion of the original "little daughter" (*thygatros*) is complicated by the later reference to *korasion* that may increase her age by a few years. Moreover, the same word, *korasion*, is used in chapter 5 to refer to Jarius's daughter, who is said to be twelve years old. Additionally, the word used for young girl, *korasion*, is the same word used in the Septuagint version of Esther to describe Esther and the other beautiful, young virgins. Janice Capel Anderson speaks to the complexity of *korasion* in determining the nature of Salome's dance:

> How does one understand the girl and her dance? How does one understand Herod and his guests' pleasure? The guests named are all elite males. Do we have a king and guests charmed by the innocent dance of his young daughter, the apple of his eye, or do we have a king and guests aroused—incestuously in the king's case—and hypnotized by an erotic dance, a young nubile body offering an apple like Eve? Readers have answered the question in both ways.[14]

Both words clearly do not describe a lusty seductress, thus eliminating the possibility that Salome was a fully grown adult woman performing a striptease. Instead, the text offers two other possibilities. *Thygatros* leads us to believe that Salome was a young, innocent daughter. The intertextuality of *korasion*, however, may lead us to believe that Salome was slightly older and

13. Ibid., 56.
14. Anderson, "Feminist Criticism," 121.

perhaps approaching puberty or marriageable age. This word, in the case of Jarius's daughter, may indicate that she was twelve, or in the case of Esther, it may indicate that she was a beautiful, young virgin. It is worth noting that there are not other descriptive words offered. She is not described as beautiful, marriageable, sexy, etc.

Whatever the case may be, the dance of a potentially twelve-year-old girl is hardly worth the scandalized reputation Salome's dance has received over the years. If Herod was sexually aroused by the dance of his adolescent ("tween" to use a contemporary term) daughter, the culpability is on him. Blaming Salome for any potential sexual arousal is not very different than blaming victims of sexual violence for being beautiful, sexy, or wearing a short skirt. What is more, however, the text never clearly indicates that Herod is aroused by the dance. The word used for the pleasure of the king and his guests is *ạrésen*. "According to many interpreters, this word does not refer to sexual pleasure. In the New Testament it refers to making someone happy, accommodating someone, or doing something that someone will approve or find pleasant."[15] The dance of the *thygatros/korasion* did nothing more than please Herod. This pleasure has no sexual connotation associated with it.

Finally, the word used for dance comes from *orchomai*, which simply means "dance." Absent from this term are any sexual connotations. In the same way that Herod bears the guilt if he is potentially aroused by the dance of a young girl, so too, must the reader bear the guilt of assuming that the dance of a young girl must be sexual, provocative, or lewd in order to please her father. I reiterate that the text does not explicitly state that Herod was anything other than pleased, delighted, amused by the dancing daughter; he was not aroused. Therefore, I would contend that heaping sexual connotations onto the dancing daughter—or even onto Herod—are indicative of faulty interpretation that only malign the reputation of the dancing daughter.

Interestingly, history supports these claims of innocence. Ross Kraemer disagrees with the implications of Salome's guilt in the death of John the Baptist based on historical claims; he notes that accounts of this narrative found in Josephus and the Gospels are "best regarded as separate narratives that both cannot and should not be amalgamated, with the conclusion that the assignment of blame to a young dancer, commonly taken to be Salome,

15. Ibid., 122.

and her mother, Herodias, is historically suspect and highly unlikely.[16] The reason for such a bold assertion is agreed upon by other scholars who claim that the majority of Mark's account is likely fictitious. In fact, it is precisely that the dance of Salome has been cited as major evidence that the story is fictitious, since many dismiss the possibility that a Herodian princess would have danced before a group of men. To do so, claims Florence Gillman, "would have placed Salome in the role of a courtesan or prostitute, the type of woman who typically provided entertainment at banquets . . . Furthermore, if it was a sensual performance the loose moral history of the Herodians would not preclude one of their princesses dancing in public."[17]

Additional historical factors that would preclude a Herodian dancing princess are the fact that first-century elite society would not permit dancing by respectable women or girls, especially royal daughters.[18] Moreover, Janice Capel Anderson astutely highlights that colonial Western interpreters sometimes have a tendency of othering "Oriental" women as exotic and immoral; they conclude that the hedonistic royals would surely celebrate the incestuous striptease of a young daughter. Such stereotyping is certainly present in the exegesis of scholars who scandalize Salome's dance. In this way, the text is reduced to a variety of literary foils. John is ascetic and holy while the Herodians are lascivious and depraved. Wealthy "Oriental" royals are corrupted by wealth, power, and lust, while the other Markan characters—namely John, Jesus, and the disciples—are poor, powerless, and asexual.

Regina Janes further notes that the Jesus Seminar represents one recent scholarly consensus because it concludes that the daughter's dance is merely "possible," and her request for an emplattered head "improbable."[19] So, history also indicates that the likelihood of Salome's dance being seductive is slim. What is more, according to the aforementioned scholars, many contend that the inclusion of Salome's dance is ahistorical from the outset. Differences in Mark and Matthew, word usage, and history lead us to conclude that Salome's dance was likely not the scandalous "dance of the seven veils" that we have witnessed in modernity. Rather, she was likely a young or barely adolescent girl who obeyed her mother. Further, her dance—and possibly the entire narrative—are fictitious historically. Before offering a

16. Kraemer, "Implicating Herodias," 322.

17. Gillman, *Herodias*, 81.

18. Anderson, "Feminist Criticism," 122.

19. Janes, "Why the Daughter," 443.

few concluding words about the possibilities of Salome's dance, I find it fitting to offer some feminist critiques of the texts. Janice Capel Anderson elaborates on the role of patriarchal constructs in understanding the text: "Both classes of readings—those that view the daughter and dance as innocent and those that view them as erotic—are male constructions of female gender: Salome, virgin and prostitute; Herodias, mother, procurer, and destroyer . . . Interpreters of this story split the 'female' into depraved mother and innocent daughter or depraved daughter as object of male desire."[20] In the same way that the seminary student who began our chapter demonized Salome as a "slut" based on his faulty and misogynistic interpretation of the text, so too do many interpreters desire to place Salome into their own binary understandings of women: virgin or whore.

What we know about Salome does not neatly place her into either category for two reasons. First, and primarily, women and girls do not always neatly fit into one of those androcentric and limited categories. This is a trend we have seen with many of the dancing women throughout this book. Second, the text actually tells us very little about the dancing daughter. The daughter and her dance are not described. Instead, both the daughter and her dance function as mirrors reflecting Herod and Herodias. The child never makes a demand on her own volition, but instead at the prodding of her mother. She mirrors her mother's desire.

The text does not describe the dance in any way. The dance does not even occupy an entire sentence. While we may not be able to describe the dance in full, the text, word usage, history, and solid feminist exegesis remind us that the dance was not likely scandalous, seductive, or sexy. Instead, it was likely similar to those early artistic renderings that were produced before the development of the femme fatal. It was likely the playful dance of a young child who wanted to please the party guests with leaps, twirls, and skips. It was likely a dance of innocence. It is dances such as this one—and the story that contains it—that have the potential to revolutionize worship today.

How Salome's Dance Can Revolutionize Worship Today

Two key concepts gleaned from Salome's story have the potential to revolutionize worship today. The first is the virtue of innocence that Salome's dance portrays. The second is the disparity between the biblical text and

20. Anderson, "Feminist Criticism," 126–127.

artistic portrayals of Salome throughout history. So, the seemingly opposi-tional principles of innocence and disparity guide this section. Let us begin with innocence.

Other dancing figures have embodied principles such as abandon and liberation that are particularly suited for the embodied practices of chil-dren in worship. Salome's dance of innocence, however, best highlights the possibilities for children to help revolutionize worship today. As mentioned in previous chapters, allowing and empowering children to lead the con-gregation in simple choreographed movement would employ both inno-cence and empowerment. It would illustrate the power of worshiping God through the eyes of a child, through the eyes of innocence. A particular example could include providing a group of children with the text from Mark or Matthew that describes Salome's story; it is likely that these chil-dren have not yet been exposed to the myriad artistic representations that malign Salome's character, so they begin with an innocent interpretation. Empower the children to read and interpret the story through their own eyes and to then depict the story as a play or in choreography in worship. Similarly, children could be provided with a variety of differing texts and asked to do the same thing. Since children do not yet have the background baggage that many adults bring to the text, they can offer fresh interpreta-tions that have the power to rid adults of their cynicism or preconceived notions regarding particularly tough passages in Scripture.

This virtue of innocence is not limited to the perspectives of children, however. I recall, for example, the way Gordan Dragt describes asking a professional choreographer to create a dance to begin the Advent season at Middle Collegiate Church in New York City.[21] As he describes the im-portance of including the arts in worship, he recounts an encounter with this choreographer. After asking her to choreograph a dance for Advent she responds, "I'd love to, but I have one question. What's Advent?" Instead of providing her with tomes of information about the history of Advent, all the Scripture that the lectionary provides for the season, or answering with a long theological explanation of Advent, Dragt instead decided that the perspective of an "outsider" was needed in order to keep the season fresh, new, and alive. In a sense, this choreographer's approach to Advent embodied the virtue of innocence. She did not bring with her any back-ground baggage or expectations of what the season—or church worship more generally—are supposed to look like. The perspectives of "outsiders"

21. Dragt, *One Foot Planted*, 98.

have the power to embody innocence in worship. They see texts, seasons, worship, and liturgy through a new, fresh, and innocent point of view. This point of view has the potential to revolutionize worship today.

While the innocence of children and the fresh perspectives of "outsiders" can help us to see worship anew, highlighting the concept of disparity may also prove evocative. On the surface these two concepts appear mutually exclusive but when working in tandem they can truly revolutionize worship. Throughout this chapter, the disparity between artistic portrayals of Salome and the biblical text's portrayal of Salome have been highlighted. Countless visual artists, playwrights, composers, choreographers, and film-makers have depicted Salome as a scandalous seductress whose titillating dance is responsible for the beheading of a beloved prophet. The biblical text, on the other hand, offers no description of Salome's dance and instead calls her a little daughter. In this manner, acknowledging the way art and popular culture influence our interpretations of Scripture is important. What might worship look like if children interpreted and staged a short play telling Salome's story while artistic images of Salome are printed on worship bulletins or projected onto a large screen? Might this lesson in contrasts and disparity teach worshipers something important about the roles of the arts, culture, and gender in understanding scriptural texts and worship and general? Likewise, imagine the possibility of having readers intersperse lines from Wilde's play or Strauss's opera when reading from Mark's or Matthew's account of Salome's story in worship.

These possibilities are not limited to Salome's story alone. Rather, the arts, culture, gender, race, class, sex, and social location all play an important role in the way we read, interpret, and portray Scripture in corporate worship. What does the text tell us about being a worshiping community? What do the artistic portrayals of the text tell us about being a worshiping community? Where is the truth in the midst of the disparity? Furthermore, where is the God we worship in the midst of the disparity? These contrasts are evocative fodder for meaningful worship. Worship is revolutionized when it is not afraid to ask difficult questions and to dwell in the inconsistencies and disparities between text and canvas, biblical story and stage. Illuminating these disparities just may awaken worshipers to the notion that we are not as innocent or as blank of a slate as we sometimes think we approach worship. Rather, each of us approaches worship, Scripture, and theology with our own lenses of interpretation and social locations. Illustrating how this occurs in a particular text—such as the ones about

Salome—may empower individuals to examine their own approaches to worship and Scripture and see what factors influence their interpretations and perspectives. Doing such would surely revolutionize worship today.

Throughout this chapter it has been my aim to counter the negative statements of that seminary student who maligned Salome's character by calling her a "slut." As we have seen, the likelihood of Salome being a wanton seductress, sensually dancing to provoke the beheading of John the Baptist is highly unlikely in the biblical text. This disparity, however, is ever-present in the ways Salome has been portrayed throughout history. Operas, plays, choreography, visual art, and film have each influenced our interpretation. The innocence of Salome's dance combines with the disparity between the biblical text and art to revolutionize our approach to worship. It is because of her dance that we may worship with the innocence of a child. And it is because of her misunderstood story that we can highlight the ways culture, art, and patriarchy influence the way we interpret Scripture and worship. As we embody both innocence and disparity in our worship, I am convinced that Salome's sullied reputation is redeemed.

CHAPTER 8

Conclusions: Jesus' Dance of Community
Acts of John 94–95

Graces dances, dance ye all
The number twelve dance on high
All on high have part in our dance
Those who dance not, know not what is to come . . .

—ACTS OF JOHN 94–95[1]

Throughout this text we have heard the stories of several biblical dancers. Their lives and dances are filled with celebration, lament, intrigue, scandal, passion, subversion, and misunderstanding. When I speak about these dancers from the pulpit, people are sometimes surprised. Much to their surprise, Scripture really is full of dancing admonitions. Rarely are worshipers more surprised than when they discover Jesus' dance from the *Acts of John* 94–95. Most people have a solid picture of Jesus in their minds—be it of a pacifist, table turner, or righteous one—and dancing is typically not part of the picture. And yet in the *Acts of John* we discover a singing and dancing Jesus who joins hands with the disciples and leads them in a circle dance. I would like to conclude that such dancing is theological and that it teaches us of the power of community.

The apocryphal *Acts of John* is commonly understood to be written around the second century CE, though scholars contest which portions are original. The *Acts of John* were deemed heretical and excluded from the canon in the eighth century at the Second Council of Nicea by the

1. My translation.

Orthodox Church due to the text's docetic tendencies. It was likely popular in the first centuries of the early church when the image of a dancing Jesus would not have seemed so surprising. And the traditional author is thought to be Leucius Charinus, a disciple of Apostle John.

The text describes how Jesus told the disciples to form a circle around him and hold hands. From the middle of the circle Jesus gives instructions for the disciples to answer "amen" as a response to his statements. He then begins to sing a hymn and dance. Max Pulver attributes this singing and dancing as a Gnostic initiation ritual.[2] Similarly, Schattenmann notes that the dance functions as a ritual ceremony parallel with the Eleusinian mysteries.[3] Arthur Dewey suggests that Jesus' dance is best classified as a *hyporchema*, which is a Hellenistic tradition involving ecstatic dance.[4] Likewise, Schneider concludes that the hymn is an initiation into gnosis via dance.[5] These scholars, while diverging on the particularities of Jesus' dance, all agree that Jesus historically danced. This is nothing short of revolutionary. They also all agree that the function of the dance was communal and ecstatic.

The *Acts of John* elevates the status of dancing by associating it with Jesus, the mind, and as a way to overcome suffering. Jesus sings the hymn and dances the circle dance following the Last Supper and prior to his arrest, trial, and crucifixion. The fact that Jesus chose to pause in the midst of his last days to sing and dance with his disciples illustrates the power and meaning embedded in the danced ritual. "One who dances not, knows not what is to come," the *Acts of John* 94 tells us. "Presumably one must dance to know, or one must know to dance . . . Those who dance with Jesus are the insiders of the knowledge. Those who do not dance are the outsiders. Assuming that this ritual was actually practiced by groups of Christians, then it follows that the dancers, those who belong to these groups, have the insiders' knowledge."[6] In this way, the dancing body is not separated from the thinking mind; rather, the two are inextricably linked. Both are pivotal parts of the Christian faith. One knows of the mysteries of Jesus via the dance. Not through reading. Not through discussion. Not through doctrine. Through dance.

2. Pulver, "Jesu Reigen," 5.

3. Schattenmann, *Studien Zum*. See also, Schneider, *The Mystery*, 3.

4. Dewey, "The Hymn," 68–80.

5. Schneider, *The Mystery*.

6. Beard-Shouse, "The Circle Dance," 22.

The *Acts of John* 101 continues with Jesus stating, "even that suffering which I showed to you and to the rest in my dance, I will that it be called a mystery." Consequently, the dance reveals the mystery of Christ's suffering. It is a way of knowing—knowing with the dancing body. The dance was a way to step into the mystery of faith. What is more, it is important to note that this was not an individual dance or a performative solo dance. It was a circle dance, a dance performed within the confines of the worshiping community. Hand-in-hand with those who believed in his message of peace, liberation, and justice, Jesus and the disciples danced. They danced for knowledge. They danced to overcome suffering. They danced amidst mystery. They danced in community. For one cannot perform a circle dance alone. Rather, one must grasp the hands of the beloved community to form a circle dance.

The image of a dancing Jesus is, indeed, revolutionary. But it is also ancient. Just because many Christians today have never thought of Jesus as a dancer does not mean that the early church did not relish this embodied image. In fact, in her fascinating book, *Dancing in the Streets: A History of Collective Joy*, Barbara Ehrenreich recounts the ways the early church associated Jesus with the ultimate lord of the dance, Dionysus.[7] Dionysus is the Greek god of the grape harvest, winemaking, ecstasy, and ritual madness who was known for inviting women and the poor into wild and equalizing dances of abandon. Ehrenreich notes the similarities of these two dancing gods, highlighting that both were fathered by a god and mothered by a woman. In the case of Jesus, the Godhead of the Trinity and Mary were his parents. In the case of Dionysus, Zeus was his father and a woman named Semele was his mother. Both were wondering charismatics who attracted women and the poor to their causes. Both Jesus and Dionysus were associated with wine and neither were ascetics. Both were seemingly asexual, or at least lacking an official consort. Both were healers and lovers of peace. Both were egalitarian. And both sang and danced. Whether it was waving one's hair in Dionysian abandon or gathering in a circle to dance a round dance, both Jesus and Dionysus were lords of the dance.

Thus, it is clear that, like the other biblical figures examined throughout this book, Jesus danced. Hand-in-hand with his disciples—his nearest and dearest friends—Jesus sang and danced during the most difficult time of his life. Leading up to his arrest, trial, and crucifixion, Jesus chose to

7. See Ehrenreich, *Dancing in the Streets*. Specifically read the chapter on Jesus as Dionysus.

dance with his disciples. One can only wonder what Christian worship and theology would look like if we celebrated the dancing and singing Jesus as frequently as we celebrated the righteous Jesus, or the healing Jesus, or the crucified Jesus. How might our worship change? How might our approach to our bodies changes? Could worship be revolutionized if we simply grasped the hands of those in our worshiping community and began to dance?

How Jesus' Dance Can Revolutionize Worship Today

The dance of Jesus in the *Acts of John* 94–95 teaches worshipers of the power of community. Physically dancing hand-in-hand with your community involves both risk and affirmation. The risk stems from our fears of vulnerability or looking foolish. What if we forget the steps? What if we stumble? The beauty and affirmation of a communal circle dance, however, is that you have the person on either side of you to help guide and support you. The individuals on either side also have their community for guidance and support. If you step to the right when everyone else steps to the left, your community will pull you in the correct direction. If you forget the steps, you can simply look around the circle and follow your community. It is a dance of reciprocity, give-and-take; it is a dance of communal affirmation.

There are a myriad of simple circle dances stemming from the history of Christian worship, along with a variety of other traditions that can be employed in worship. Partnering a well-known hymn, such as "Gift to Be Simple," with a simple circle dance can empower the community to affirm and celebrate their bodies as good, worthy, and beloved rather than objects of shame. Forming an inner circle that holds hands and repeatedly steps to the right while an outer circle holds hands and repeatedly steps to the left invokes a sense of unity and community. It also invokes both the circle dance from the *Acts of John* and the ring shout tradition from the hush/brush harbors of the "invisible institution" of slave worship.[8] Similarly, a spiral dance can be employed to evoke unity and community, as well. In a spiral dance, the congregation forms a circle by holding hands. The leader of the spiral dance lets go of the hand of one person; this person becomes the end of the spiral. The leader then proceeds to walk inside the circle, pulling the hand of the person behind to follow. Circling inward deeper and deeper until you can go no farther, the leader then reverses and begins

8. For more on the ring shout, see Raboteau, *Slave Religion* or Floyd, "Ring Shout!"

to circle outward, continuing to pull the hand of the person behind. As you spiral inward and outward, you are face-to-face with almost every person in the circle. The spiral dance, then, is a perfect example of community-building and unity in a manner similar to the circle dance employed in the *Acts of John*. What is more, both of the simple circle dances I described can be shared by people from an array of ages and physical abilities. I have performed the spiral dance with a baby in a stroller as part of the circle and with a person in a wheelchair holding the hands of the community. I have shared the simple inner and outer circle dance with people ranging in age from two to ninety-five. Thus, the notion of community and unity is not limited by age or ability but extends to the entire worshiping community.

If the congregation is already familiar with some simple circle danc-ing, introducing ones that are still fairly simple but have slightly more com-plex choreography is also a revolutionary way to build community, unity, and affirm the body. Many circle dances from the Israeli folk dance tradi-tion are perfect examples of this. In no way do I propose that Christians should appropriate these dances, but instead one could teach some of the fascinating history of Israeli folk dance[9] and choose dances that stem from interpretations of the Hebrew Bible since it is a text shared by both Jews and Christians. One of the primary intentions in the formation of Israeli folk dance was building community, after all.

A classic example of an Israeli folk dance that builds community and stems from the Hebrew Bible is *Mayim Mayim*, which translates as "water water" and is inspired by Isaiah's prophecy to "draw water with joy out of the wells of salvation." Beginning with the traditional grapevine, the danc-ers moved left, their right leg crossing front, stepping side, and then right leg crossing behind. After four sets of grapevines, the group begins the of-ficial "mayim" section of the dance. With gusto, the entire group bounds toward the inside of the circle with four running steps while gradually rais-ing their arms and singing "*Mayim Mayim Mayim Mayim*." They then take four steps back while lowering their arms and repeat the "center and back" pattern once again. Still holding hands in solidarity, next they hop on their right foot while their left heel touches across and then to the left side; fac-ing center, this is repeated three more times. After repeating all these steps throughout the dance, as the song draws to a close, the dancers clap their

---

9. I detail the fascinating history of Israeli folk dance in my book *Embodying the Feminine in the Dances of the World's Religions*.

hands overhead on the final hops. *Mayim Mayim* is a classic example of how to share a meaningful circle dance that can create community.

In addition to sharing a variety of different circle dances in worship, the concept of a dancing Jesus can also be evoked in music and visual art. Can you imagine how unifying and celebratory worship could be if you read the *Acts of John* 94–95, danced a circle dance, portrayed images of a dancing Jesus on a screen or bulletin covers, and sang "Lord of the Dance"? Worship could truly be revolutionized in creative and embodied ways by singing the lyrics below while performing a simple circle dance in community:

> *I danced in the morning when the world was begun*
> *And I danced in the moon and the stars and the sun*
> *And I came down from heaven and I danced on the earth*
> *At Bethlehem I had my birth*
> *Dance, then, wherever you may be*
> *I am the Lord of the Dance, said he*
> *And I'll lead you all wherever you may be*
> *And I'll lead you all in the dance, said he*
> *I danced for the scribe and the Pharisee*
> *But they would not dance and they would not follow me*
> *I danced for the fishermen, for James and John*
> *They came to me and the dance went on*
> *I danced on the Sabbath when I cured the lame*
> *The holy people said it was a shame*
> *They whipped and they stripped and they hung me high*
> *And they left me there on a cross to die*
> *I danced on a Friday and the sky turned black*
> *It's hard to dance with the devil on your back*
> *They buried my body and they thought I'd gone*
> *But I am the dance and I still go on*
> *They cut me down and I leapt up high*
> *I am the life that'll never, never die*
> *I'll live in you if you'll live in me*
> *I am the Lord of the Dance, said he*[10]

10. Carter, "Lord of the Dance." 1963.

When ideologies and doctrines often divide communities, joining hand-in-hand in a simple circle dance unites body, mind, and heart in an act of embodied worship. Such worship echoes the communal power of Jesus' dance from the *Acts of John* 94–95. It creates a sense of unity and community. Such communal dancing has the power to revolutionize worship today.

Conclusions: How Biblical Dancers Can Revolutionize Worship

Over the course of this book, we have stepped inside the lives of seven dancing figures from Scripture. Their stories, like their dances, are filled liberation and bondage, celebration and lament, ecstasy and abandon, passion and sensuality, victory and subversion, community and unity. Some of the dancers, such as Judith and Jesus, are paragons of virtue. Some of the dancers, such as David and the Shulamite, have stories and dances riddled with the complexity of eros, passion, and sexuality. Some of the dancers, such as Jephthah's daughter and Salome, are misunderstood, maligned, and sacrificed. And some of the dancers, such as Miriam, are examples of how the body expresses the unfettered joy of worshiping a God of liberation. All of these dances have the power to revolutionize worship today.

The dances we have uncovered cannot be separated from the contexts of the dancer's lives and stories. Would Miriam's dance truly embody liberation if we did not know that her people had previously been in bondage? Could Jephthah's daughter's dance truly embody lament if we did not know her father's faithless vow to sacrifice her as a burnt offering? Would David's dance truly embody abandon if we were not aware of the complex relationships between him and his wife, his community, and his God? Could the Shulamite's dance truly embody passion if we did not translate the erotic love poem that encompasses her sensual dance? Would Judith's dance truly embody subversion if we did not grasp the nuances of how she overturned patriarchal systems that boxed widows, women, and warriors into binary and gendered categories? Could Salome's dance truly embody innocence if we simply allowed artists and popular culture to interpret the text for us rather than understanding what Salome's dance really looked like? Would Jesus' dance truly embody community if we continued to confine Jesus into the images tradition has given us?

These self-evident questions lead to an array of other questions about the power of the dancing body to revolutionize worship today. It is my hope that these questions will embolden you to examine the way you worship, the way your community worships, and the way your tradition worships. What kind of theology does our church espouse if the body is rarely affirmed or celebrated in worship? What does worship teach us about God if worship is confined to the head, heart, and voice alone? What does worship teach us about the worth and dignity of humans if worship is confined to head, heart, and voice alone? What does worship teach us about our approach to Scripture if we rarely read, preach from, or sing about the texts highlighted throughout this book?

I do not propose to give you answers to these questions. Rather, I hope that you will allow the powerful and revolutionaries stories of the biblical dancers that have filled this book to answer them for you. I hope that you are empowered to implement some of these revolutionary steps into your individual and corporate worship. In so doing, I hope your body and the bodies in your faith community can be redeemed, celebrated, and affirmed as worthy, beautiful, and beloved. It is my hope the dances of these seven biblical figures inspires you to shift the questions you're asking about the way you worship, the way your community worships, and the way your tradition worships. In these ways, you may be emboldened to ask, what kind of theology does our church espouse when the body is affirmed and celebrated in worship through dance and embodied rituals? What does worship teach us about God and humanity when worshiping bodies dance, pray, sing, sway, clap, bow, kneel, touch, and lift hands? What does worship teach us about our approach to Scripture when we uncover hidden texts, proclaim forgotten stories from the pulpit, and sing and dance the texts that describe the dances of Miriam, Jephthah's daughter, David, the Shulamite, Judith, Salome, and Jesus?

Remember that revolution does not come quickly or easily. It takes time, intentionality, thoughtfulness, and the telling of difficult stories. Incorporating the virtues taught by these dancing biblical figures into the life and worship of your church will also take time, intentionality, thoughtfulness, and the telling of difficult stories. Partner these dancing stories with the stories of individuals in your congregation. Miriam may dance alongside of a person in your congregation who has experienced God's liberation out of the bondage of trafficking, an abusive job, or as a refugee. Jephthah's daughter may dance alongside of a person who has experienced domestic violence, a mother who has lost a child to war or gang violence, or a child of an abusive parent. David may dance alongside of person who has experienced the wild abandon of worship, trance, or ritual from another culture or tradition. The Shulamite may dance alongside of LGBTQ persons in the community who have previously been shunned or rejected and now find themselves affirmed by a holy community who loves them. Judith may dance alongside of another beautiful, brainy, faithful feminist in the congregation who has subverted patriarchal systems by finding affirmation in the workplace. Salome may dance alongside of a person whose reputation has been maligned by people unwilling to hear and learn the truth of their difficult story. And Jesus dances alongside of us all, hand-in-hand with our dancing community.

Whatever and wherever you evoke the stories of the biblical dancers, I am confident that revolution will soon follow. As you dance, remember that your footsteps tread through a history of liberation, lament, abandon, passion, subversion, innocence, and community. And when you experience these myriad virtues, I hope that your body will respond by dancing. After all, if I can't dance, I don't want to be a part of your revolution.

Bibliography

Ackerman, Susan. *Warrior, Dancer, Seductress, Queen: Women in Judges and Biblical Israel.* New York: Doubleday, 1998.

———. *When Heroes Love: the Ambiguity of Eros in the Stories of Gilgamesh and David.* New York: Columbia University Press, 2005.

Albright, W. F. "Archaic Survivals in the Text of Canticles." In *Hebrew and Semitic Studies Presented to G. R. Driver,* edited by D. Winton Thomas and W. D. McHardy, 1–7. Oxford: Clarendon, 1963.

Al-Rawi, Rosina-Fawzia. *Grandmother's Secrets: The Ancient Rituals and Healing Power of Belly Dancing.* Translated by Monique Arav. Northampton, MA: Interlink, 2000.

Alter, Robert. *The Art of Biblical Narrative.* New York: Basic, 1981.

Anderson, Janice Capel. "Feminist Criticism: The Dancing Daughter." In *Mark and Method,* edited by Janice Capel Anderson and Stephen Moore, 111–44. Minneapolis: Fortress, 1992.

Anderson, Janice Capel, and Stephen Moore, eds. *Mark and Method: New Approaches in Biblical Studies.* Minneapolis: Fortress, 1992.

Apostolos-Cappadona, Diane. "By the Hand of a Woman." In *Art as Religious Studies,* edited by Doug Adams and Diane Apostolos-Cappadona, 81–97. New York: Crossroads, 1990.

———. "Martha Graham and the Quest for the Feminine in Eve, Lilith, and Judith." In *Art as Religious Studies,* edited by Doug Adams and Diane Apostolos-Cappadona, 118–33. New York: Crossroads, 1990.

———. "Scriptural Women Who Danced." In *Dance As Religious Studies,* edited by Doug Adams and Diane Apostolos-Cappadona, 95–108. New York: Crossroads, 1990.

———, and Doug Adams, eds. *Dance as Religious Studies.* New York: Crossroads, 1993.

Bach, Alice, ed. *The Pleasures of Her Text, Feminist Readings of Biblical and Historical Texts.* Valley Forge, PA: Trinity, 1991.

Bailey, Randall. *David in Love and War.* Sheffield, UK: Sheffield Academic, 1990.

Beard-Shouse, Melody. "The Circle Dance of the Cross in the Acts of John: An Early Christian Ritual." Master's thesis, University of Kansas, 2010.

Bentley, Toni. *Sisters of Salome.* New Haven, CT: Yale University Press, 2002.

Black, Fiona. "Unlikely Bedfellows: Allegorical and Feminist Readings of Song of Songs 7:1-8," in *The Song of Songs: A Feminist Companion to the Bible,* edited by Athalya Brenner and Carole R. Fontaine, 104–29. Sheffield, UK: Sheffield Academic, 2000.

Boer, Roland. *Knockin' on Heaven's Door: The Bible and Popular Culture.* New York: Routledge, 1999.

———. "Night Sprinkle(s): Pornography and the Song of Songs." In *Knockin' on Heaven's Door*, 53–70. New York: Routledge, 1999.

Brenner, Athalya. "'Come Back, Come Back The Shulammite' (Song of Songs 7.1–10): A Parody of the *Wasf* Genre." In *On Humour and the Comic in the Hebrew Bible*, edited by Yehuda Radday and Athalya Brenner, 251–76. Sheffield, UK: Almond, 1990.

———. "Gazing Back at the Shulammite, Yet Again." *Biblical Interpretation* 11/3 (2003) 295–300.

———. *I Am . . . Biblical Women Tell Their Own Stories*. Minneapolis: Fortress, 2005.

———, ed. *A Feminist Companion to Esther, Judith and Susanna*. Sheffield, UK: Sheffield Academic, 1995.

———, ed. *On Humor and the Comic in the Hebrew Bible*. Sheffield, UK: Almond, 1990.

———, ed. *The Song of Songs: A Feminist Companion to the Bible*. Sheffield, UK: Sheffield Academic, 1989.

Broner, W. M., and Naomi Nimrod. *The Women's Haggadah*. San Francisco: Harper, 1994.

Brueggemann, Walter. "Exodus." In *The New Interpreter's Bible: A Commentary in Twelve Volumes*, edited by Leander Keck, vol. 1. Nashville: Abingdon, 1994.

Buonaventura, Wendy. *Belly Dancing: The Serpent and the Sphinx*. London: Virago, 1983.

———. *Serpent of the Nile: Women and Dance in the Arab World*. Northampton, MA: Interlink, 1998.

Burrus, Virginia, and Stephen Moore. "Unsafe Sex: Feminism, Pornography, and the Song of Songs." *Biblical Interpretations* 11/1 (2003) 24–52.

Clines, David, and Tamara Eskenazi, eds. *Telling Queen Michal's Story: An Experiment in Comparative Interpretation*. Edinburgh: T. & T. Clark, 2009.

Cohen, Norman. "Miriam's Song: A Modern Midrashic Reading." *Judaism* 33/2 (Spring 1984) 179-190.

Coluccia, Pina, Anette Paffrath, and Jean Pütz. *Belly Dancing: The Sensual Art of Energy and Spirit*. Rochester, VT: Park Street, 2003.

Craven, Toni. "Artistry and Faith in the Book of Judith." PhD diss., Vanderbilt University, 1980.

———. "The Book of Judith in the Context of Twentieth-Century Studies of the Apocryphal/Deuterocanonical Books." *Currents in Biblical Research* 1/2 (April 2003) 187–229.

———. "Convention and Tradition in the Book of Judith." *Semeia* 28 (1983) 49–61.

———. "Women Who Lied for the Faith." In *Justice and the Holy: Essays in Honor of Walter Harrelson*, edited by P. Paris and D. Knight, 35–49. Atlanta: Scholars, 1989.

Crosby, Janice. "The Goddess Dances: Spirituality and American Women's Interpretations of Middle Eastern Dance." In *Daughters of the Goddess: Studies of Identity, Healing, and Empowerment*, edited by Wendy Griffin, 166–82. Oxford: Altamira, 2000.

Deen, Edith. *Wisdom from Women in the Bible*. New York: Harper & Row, 1978.

DeSola, Carla. *The Spirit Moves: A Handbook of Dance and Prayer*. Washington, DC: Liturgical Conference, 1977.

Dewey, Arthur. "The Hymn in the *Acts of John*: Dance as Hermeneutic." *Semeia* 38 (1986) 67–80.

Dinicu, Carolina Varga. "Belly Dancing and Childbirth." *Dance Pages Magazine* (Winter 1984) 53–65.

Douglas-Klotz, Neil. *Desert Wisdom: Sacred Middle Eastern Writings from the Goddess through the Sufis*. San Francisco: Harper, 1995.

Dragt, Gordan. *One Foot Planted in the Center, the Other Dangling off the Edge: How Intentional Leadership Can Transform Your Church.* Salt Lake City: Millennial Mind, 2009.

Dundes, Alan. "Comment on 'Narrative Structures in the Book of Judith.'" In *Narrative Structures in the Book of Judith: Protocol of the Eleventh Colloquy, 27 January [i.e. 17 March] 1974,* edited by Luis Alonso-Schökel and W. Wuellner, 27–29. Berkeley, CA: The Center for Hermeneutical Studies in Hellenistic and Modern Culture, 1975.

Ehrenreich, Barbara. *Dancing in the Streets: A History of Collective Joy.* New York: Metropolitan, 2007.

Fennema, Sharon. "Falling All Around Me: Worship Performing Theodicy in the Midst of the San Francisco AIDS Crisis." PhD diss., Graduate Theological Union, 2011.

Feyerabend, Karl. *Langenscheidt's Pocket Hebrew Dictionary.* 15th ed. Berlin: Langenscheidt, 1992.

Floyd, Samuel, Jr. "Ring Shout! Literary Studies, Historical Studies, and Black Music Inquiry." *Black Music Research Journal* 22/1 (Spring 2002) 49–70.

Frankel, Ellen. *The Five Books of Miriam.* New York: Putnam, 1996.

Fuchs, Esther. "Marginalization, Ambiguity, Silencing: The Story of Jephthah's Daughter." *Journal of Feminist Studies in Religion* 5/1 (May 2001) 35–45.

Gillman, Florence Morgan. *Herodias: At Home in That Fox's Den.* Collegeville, MN: Liturgical, 2003.

Gioseffi, Daniela. *Earth Dancing: Mother Nature's Oldest Rite.* Harrisburg, PA: Stackpole, 1980.

Goettner-Abendroth, Heide. *The Dancing Goddess: Principles of a Matriarchal Aesthetic.* Boston: Beacon, 1992.

Graves, Robert. *Greek Myths.* London: Penguin, 1992.

Griffin, Wendy, ed. *Daughters of the Goddess: Studies of Healing, Identity, and Empowerment.* Walnut Creek, CA: AltaMira, 2000.

Gruber, Mayer. "Ten Dance-Derived Expressions in the Hebrew Bible." In *Dance as Religious Studies,* edited by Doug Adams and Diane Apostolos-Cappadona, 48–67. New York: Crossroads, 1990.

Gunn, David. *Judges.* Blackwell Bible Commentaries. Malden, MA: Blackwell, 2005.

Hamlin, John. *Judges: At Risk in the Promise Land.* Grand Rapids: Eerdmans, 1990.

Hammer, Jill. *Sisters at Sinai: New Tales of Biblical Women.* Philadelphia: Jewish Publication Society, 2001.

Henry, Matthew. *Matthew Henry's Commentary on the Whole Bible.* Vol. 2, *Joshua to Esther.* New York: Revell, 1935. Online: http://www.ccel.org/ccel/henry/mhc2.iiSam.vii.html.

Hibbert, Vivian. *Prophetic Worship: Releasing the Presence of God.* Dallas: Cuington, 1999.

Hobin, Tina. *Belly Dance: The Dance of Mother Earth.* London: Marion Boyars, 2003.

Hospodar de Kornitz, Blaise. *Salome: Virgin or Prostitute?* New York: Pageant, 1953.

Jacobus, Mary, ed. *Reading Women: Essays in Feminist Criticism.* New York: Columbia University Press, 1986.

Janes, Regina. "Why the Daughter of Herodias Must Dance." *Journal for the Study of the New Testament* 28/4 (June 2006) 443–67.

Karayanni, Stavros Stavrou. *Dancing Fear and Desire: Race, Sexuality and Imperial Politics in Middle Eastern Dance.* Waterloo, ON: Wilfrid Laurier University Press, 2004.

———. "Performing 'Sex,' Race, and Nation: Middle Eastern Dance and the Politics of Empire." PhD diss., University of Calgary, 2002.

Kraemer, Ross. "Implicating Herodias and Her Daughter in the Death of John the Baptizer: A Christian Theological Strategy?" *Journal of Biblical Literature* 125/2 (Summer 2006) 321–49.

Levine, Amy-Jill. "Sacrifice and Salvation: Otherness and Domestication in the Book of Judith." In *A Feminist Companion to Esther, Judith and Susanna*, edited by Athalya Brenner, 208–23. Sheffield, UK: Sheffield Academic, 1995.

Longman, Tremper, III. *Song of Songs*. New International Commentary on the Old Testament. Grand Rapids: Eerdmans, 2001.

Manor, Giora. *The Gospel According to Dance: Choreography and the Bible from Ballet to Modern*. New York: St. Martin's, 1980.

Meyers, Carol, et al., eds. *Women in Scripture: A Dictionary of Named and Unnamed Women in the Hebrew Bible, the Apocryphal/Deuterocanonical Books and New Testament*. New York: Houghton Mifflin, 2000.

Miller, R. H. "Liturgical Materials in the Acts of John." *Studia Patristica* 13 (1975) 375–81.

Mirkin, Marsha. *The Women Who Danced By the Sea: Finding Ourselves in the Stories of Our Biblical Foremothers*. Rhinebeck, NY: Monkfish, 2004.

Moore, Carey A. *Judith: A New Translation with Introduction and Commentary*. New York: Doubleday, 1985.

Moore, Stephen. "The Song of Songs in the History of Sexuality." *The American Society of Church History* 69/2 (June 2000) 328–49.

Morgenstern, Julian. "The Etymological History of the Three Hebrew Synonyms for 'To Dance.'" *American Oriental Society Journal* 36 (1916) 321–32.

Neumann, Erich. *The Great Mother*. London: Olten, 1974.

Nieuwkerk, Karin. *A Trade Like Any Other: Female Singers and Dancers in Egypt*. Austin: University of Texas Press, 1995.

Ohanian, Armên. *La Danseuse de Shamakha*. Paris: B. Grasset, 1918.

———. *Les rires d'une charmeuse de serpents*. Paris: Les Revues, 1931.

Paris, Peter, and Douglas Knight, eds. *Justice and the Holy: Essays in Honor of Walter Harrelson*. Atlanta: Scholars, 1989.

Patterson, Barbara A. B. "Redeemed Bodies: Fullness of Life." In *Human Disability and the Service of God*, edited by Nancy L. Eiseland and Don E. Saliers, 123–43. Nashville: Abingdon, 1998.

Pope, Marvin. *The Anchor Bible: Song of Songs*. Garden City, NY: Doubleday, 1977.

Propp, William. *Exodus 1–18*. Anchor Bible Commentary. New York: Doubleday, 1999.

Pulver, Max. "Jesu Reigen Und Kreuzigung Nach Den Johannesakten." *Eranos Jahrbuch* 9 (1942) 141–78.

Raboteau, Albert. *Slave Religion: The "Invisible Institution" in the Antebellum South*. Oxford: Oxford University Press, 2004.

Redmond, Layne. *When the Drummers Were Women: A Spiritual History of Women*. New York: Three Rivers, 1997.

Ringgren, H. "הלל." In *Theological Dictionary of the Old Testament*, edited by G. Johannes Botterweck, Helmer Ringgren, and Heinz-Josef Fabry, 3:404–10. Grand Rapids: Eerdmans, 2004.

Rock, Judith, and Norman Mealey. *Performer as Priest and Prophet: Restoring the Intuitive in Worship through Music and Dance*. New York: HarperCollins, 1988.

Rosenstock, Bruce. "David's Play: Fertility Rituals and the Glory of God in 2 Samuel 6." *Journal for the Study of the Old Testament* 31/1 (2006) 63–80.

Sawyer, Deborah. "Dressing Up/Dressing Down: Power, Performance and Identity in the Book of Judith." *Theology and Sexuality* 15 (2001) 2–31.

Schattenmann, Johannes. *Studien Zum Neutestamentlichen Prosahymnus.* Munich: Beck, 1965.

Schneider, Paul. *The Mystery of the Acts of John.* San Francisco: Mellen Research, 1991.

Schussler Fiorenza, Elisabeth, ed. *Searching the Scriptures, vol. 2: A Feminist Commentary.* New York: Crossroads, 1994.

Seow, Choon Leong. *Myth, Drama, and the Politics of David's Dance.* Atlanta: Scholars, 1989.

Sharif, Keti. *Bellydance: A Guide to Middle Eastern Dance: Its Music, Its Culture and Costume.* Crows Nest, Australia: Allen and Unwin, 2004.

Sonbol, Amira, ed. *Beyond the Exotic: Women's Histories in Islamic Societies.* Syracuse, NY: Syracuse University Press, 2005.

Spence, H. D. M., and Joseph Excell, eds. *The Pulpit Commentary: The Gospel according to Matthew.* Chicago: Wilcox and Follett, 1909.

Stewart, Iris. *Sacred Woman, Sacred Dance: Awakening Spirituality through Movement and Ritual.* Rochester, VT: Inner Traditions, 2000.

Stocker, Margarita. *Judith: Sexual Warrior: Women and Power in Western Culture.* New Haven, CT: Yale University Press,1998.

Strova, Maria. *The Secret Language of Belly Dancing.* Charleston, SC: Booksurge, 2006.

Trible, Phyllis. "Bringing Miriam Out of the Shadows." *Bible Review* 5 (1989) 14–25.

———. "Miriam 1." In *Women in Scripture*, edited by Carol Meyers et al., 127–29. New York: Houghton Mifflin, 2000.

———. *Texts of Terror: Literary-Feminist Reading of Biblical Narratives.* Philadelphia: Fortress, 1984.

Van Henten, Jan Willem. "Judith as Alternative Leader: A Rereading of Judith 7-13." In *A Feminist Companion to Esther, Judith and Susanna*, edited by Athalya Brenner, 224–52. Sheffield, UK: Sheffield Academic, 1995.

VanderKam, James, ed. *No One Spoke Ill of Her: Essays on Judith.* Atlanta: Scholars, 1992.

Vander Stichele, Caroline. "Murderous Mother, Ditto Daughter." *Lectio Difficilior: European Electronic Journal for Feminist Exegesis* 2 (2001) n.p. http://www.lectio.unibe.ch/01_2/v.htm.

Varga-Dinicu, Carolina. "A Criticism of Nadia Gamal." *Arabesque* (March/April 1977) 22.

Walker, Barbara. *The Woman's Dictionary of Symbols and Sacred Objects.* San Francisco: HarperSanFrancisco, 1988.

White, Ellen. "Michal the Misinterpreted." *Journal for the Study of the Old Testament* 31/4 (2007) 451–64.

Yarber, Angela. *Embodying the Feminine in the Dances of the World's Religions.* New York: Peter Lang, 2011.

———. *The Gendered Pulpit: Sex, Body, and Desire in Preaching and Worship.* Cleveland: Parson's Porch, 2013.